KU-498-866

Mitchell Symons was born in London and educated at Mill Hill School and the LSE, where he studied law. Since leaving BBC TV, where he was a researcher and then a director, he has worked as a writer, broadcaster and journalist. He was a principal writer of early editions of the board game Trivial Pursuit and has devised many television formats. He is also the author of more than forty books, and currently writes a weekly column for the Sunday Express. *Why Eating Bogeys Is Good For You* won the Blue Peter Best Book with Facts Award in 2010 and he repeated this success with *Do Igloos Have Loos?* in 2011.

www.**grossbooks**.co.uk

How much yucky stuff do you know?

Collect all these gross facts books by Mitchell Symons!

☐

☐

☐

☐

☐

☐

☐

Available now!

On your FARTS Get set, GO!

Mitchell Symons

DOUBLEDAY

ON YOUR FARTS, GET SET, GO!
A DOUBLEDAY BOOK 978 0 385 61865 6

Published in Great Britain by Doubleday,
an imprint of Random House Children's Books
A Random House Group Company

This edition published 2011

1 3 5 7 9 10 8 6 4 2

RANDOM HOUSE CHILDREN'S BOOKS
61–63 Uxbridge Road, London W5 5SA

www.kidsatrandomhouse.co.uk
www.totallyrandombooks.co.uk
www.randomhouse.co.uk

Addresses for companies within The Random House Group Limited can be
found at: www.randomhouse.co.uk/offices.htm

THE RANDOM HOUSE GROUP Limited Reg. No. 954009

A CIP catalogue record for this book is available from the British Library.

Printed and bound in Great Britain by Clays Ltd, St Ives plc

To anyone who has ever
finished well and truly last in a race.
The author knows how you feel.

Introduction

Hello, and welcome to the latest book in the series that started all those years ago with *How to Avoid a Wombat's Bum*. That's its title, but when I'm discussing it with my (wonderful, fabulous, talented, etc., etc.) editor, Lauren, we just call it *Bum* for short. The fact is, we're obliged to shorten the titles because otherwise our telephone conversations would go on for ever – instead of just for two hours at a time (no exaggeration).

So, on the same basis, *Why Eating Bogeys Is Good for You* becomes *Bogeys*, *How Much Poo Does an Elephant Do?* is *Poo*, *Why Do Farts Smell Like Rotten Eggs?* is *Farts*, *Why Does Ear Wax Taste So Gross?* is *Ear Wax*, *Why You Need a Passport When You're Going to Puke* becomes *Puke*, and *Do Igloos Have Loos?* is *Loos*. In other words, like a pair of four-year-olds, we find the naughtiest word in a phrase and ignore all the others.

This leads to conversations like:

Lauren: 'Didn't we do this in *Puke*?'

Me: 'No, we were going to put it in *Poo* but then we thought it would work better in *Farts*. In the end, it didn't make it into either.'

Lauren: 'But there's something like it in *Bogeys* or *Bum* . . .'

Me: 'No, you're thinking of *Ear Wax*.'

No wonder people who overhear our conversations think we've got potty-mouths!

By the way, do you know what an editor actually does? No, me neither. But if you find out, do please go to my website and let me know (only kidding, Lauren!)

This book has more in common with *Why You Need a Passport When You're Going to Puke* (sorry, *Puke*), than it has with *Bum, Bogeys, Farts, Ear Wax* and *Loos* – all of which were either trivia books or question-and-answer books. *Puke* was the first in the series to be devoted to a single subject (geography); this is the second, and, as you might have guessed, it's filled with facts and anecdotes about sport.

As far as I'm concerned, there's a big difference between geography and sport (yes, I know, I know, but please bear with me). I know absolutely nothing about geography – well, I didn't until I wrote the book (it's one way to learn) – but when it comes to sport, I'm a bit of a know-all. I love sport. No that's not strong enough . . . I *adore* sport and have done so ever since I can remember. Cricket, rugby union, football and tennis are my favourites – probably in that order. That's not to say I'm any good at them.

Even when I was younger and fitter, I was still not much of a sportsman. At school I was (almost) always one of the last to be picked for the team, and that carried on into my adult life. The telephone call from a rugby or a cricket captain asking me to make up the numbers – 'Honestly, Mitch, I wouldn't be bothering you but I've tried everyone else' – was a regular occurrence in my twenties. But I didn't mind: I was only too thrilled to be asked at all.

Yup, that's how much of a sports nut I was.

Now that my sporting activity is limited to swimming, table tennis and the occasional game of tennis, I'm no less passionate about sports, but I follow them on TV or in the newspapers. I also love reading books about sport . . . and now, at last, I've written my own!

The most important thing to say is that this is *not* a book for other sports nuts (though hopefully they'll enjoy it too!); instead, it's a book that *anyone* – sporty or non-sporty – can read. That's why I've filled it with great stories from the world of sport: *everyone* loves great stories!

As for the rather naughty title, this was inspired by something a friend told me many years ago. At his school sports day, his teacher used to start the races with a starting pistol. So far, nothing remarkable. However, in one race, as the boys were just about to set off, one of them did this very loud fart... at which point all the other competitors, thinking it was the starting pistol, set off on the race. It was only a sprint and they'd nearly completed it by the time the teacher had called them all back. Truly, On Your Farts, Get Set, Go!

Now for some important acknowledgements. Lauren Buckland, whom I've already mentioned, did a fantastic job on the editing, while Annie Eaton is the loveliest publisher in the world. Penny, Jack and Charlie Symons all helped enormously with the research, and if you like the look of the book (as I really do!), then it's all thanks to the designers, Dominica Clements and Nigel Baines.

In addition, I'd also like to thank the following people for their help, contributions and/or support: Gilly Adams, Luigi Bonomi, Paul Donnelley, Jonathan Fingerhut, Jenny Garrison, Bryn Musson, Nicholas Ridge, Mari Roberts, Jack Symons, Louise Symons, Martin Townsend, Clair Woodward and Rob Woolley.

If I've missed anyone out, then please know that – as with any mistakes in the book – it is, as ever, entirely down to my own stupidity.

Mitchell Symons

www.mitchellsymons.co.uk

That's interesting (1)

Richard Williams survived the sinking of
the *Titanic* in 1912 and went on to win the
Wimbledon men's doubles title in 1920.

The Marylebone Cricket Club (MCC) used to represent England in overseas cricket matches. Its first overseas fixture was to be in 1789 against France, but that unfortunately coincided with the French Revolution. However, the match wasn't totally abandoned – just postponed . . . for 200 years. So in 1989 they finally played the game and the French won by seven wickets.

From a complete stop, a human is capable of outrunning a Formula One racing car for about 10 metres. That's because a person can accelerate quicker than a car over such a short distance.

If you hit a bad shot on the tee of the first hole in a game of golf, your opponent might be kind enough to offer you a 'mulligan'. In golf, a mulligan is a retaken shot on the first tee – and *only* on the first tee – after a bad shot.

As every snooker fan knows, 147 is the magic number in snooker as it is the maximum break (15 reds, each followed by the black, and then all the colours). In fact, with free balls after a foul shot, 155 is technically the highest score possible, but the highest break ever recorded was 151 by Cliff Thorburn, who achieved his score with the benefit of a foul shot from his opponent.

The Czech team that reached the 1934 football World Cup final contained players from just two clubs.

C. B. Fry must surely lay claim to being the greatest sporting all-rounder. He captained England at cricket, played football for England and held the world long-jump record. After retiring from sport, in 1920 he was offered the throne of Albania but turned it down!

When the Olympics were held in France, in 1900, the winners were given a valuable piece of art instead of a medal.

In 1922 the great American golfer Walter Hagen arrived at Sandwich, Kent, for the Open Championship – only to discover that, as a professional, he wasn't allowed to change or eat in the clubhouse (that 'honour' was reserved for the amateur competitors – i.e. those players who weren't paid to play). So Hagen hired a stretch limousine, parked it in front of the clubhouse and used it for changing and eating.

It obviously didn't do him any harm as he won the event. At the presentation ceremony he looked at the amount on the cheque

– and, decidedly unimpressed, promptly handed it to his caddie. Hagen had the last laugh as he became golf's first millionaire.

68 per cent of professional hockey players have lost at least one tooth.

Geoffrey Boycott once batted on all five days of a Test match. In a 1977 match against Australia he began his first innings at 6.17 on the first evening and batted through the second day before being out (for 107) at 12.45 p.m. on the third day. He began his second innings at 6.05 on the fourth evening, and when England completed a seven-wicket victory at 4.42 p.m. on the fifth day, he was still at the wicket.

Other players who have matched Boycott's achievement include England's Allan Lamb and Andrew Flintoff.

In boxing, before 1900 prize fights lasted up to 100 rounds. Nowadays they're 15 rounds at most, but usually just 12 (each lasting three minutes).

Only 13 bowlers have taken a wicket with their very first ball in Test cricket. However, over 100 bowlers have taken a wicket with their very last ball in Test cricket. No bowler appears on both lists!

The US diver Harry Prieste got more enjoyment out of his Olympic medal than any other medallist . . . well, he certainly enjoyed it the longest. Born in 1896, he won the bronze medal in platform diving at the 1920 Games in Antwerp. He then lived for another 81 years – dying in 2001 at the age of 104.

At the opposite end of that scale was the Swiss rower Gottfried Kottmann. At the 1964 Tokyo Games he won the bronze medal in the single sculls rowing event on his 32nd birthday. However, just 22 days later he died in a car accident.

In 2005 a British man named Dave Cornthwaite took up skateboarding. The following year he became the first person to skate from John o'Groats (at the top of Scotland) to Land's End (at the bottom of England).

During the first few modern Olympic Games, the marathon course was an approximate distance. In 1908 the British royal family requested that it start at Windsor Castle so that the royal children could watch. The distance from Windsor Castle to the Olympic Stadium was 42,195 metres (or 26 miles and 385 yards). And that's why this is now the standard length of a marathon!

The skeleton bob race is probably one of the scariest sporting activities known to man. These sleds have no brakes and no steering wheel and fly down the track at up to 85 mph. The only way to stop is to run out of slope or to crash into something.

Wayne Rooney is extremely popular in China, where his name means 'silly nun' in Chinese characters. Incidentally, Wayne is not the only great sportsman in his family's history: he's a (distant) descendant of Bob Fitzsimmons, the 19th-century world heavyweight boxing champion.

The greatest comeback of all time?

When England won the 1966 football World Cup – yes, my friends, there was a time when we were the best team in the world – they played Portugal in the semi-finals. With Eusebio in their team, the Portuguese were formidable opponents, but they only got to the semi-finals after an extraordinary comeback against North Korea. The underdog North Koreans were 3–0 up after just 24 minutes, and it looked like a huge giant-killing feat was going to take place. But Eusebio scored four goals to help his team recover from 3–0 down to win 5–3.

Pretty incredible, huh? But not as amazing as this comeback. In April 2010 Arsenal were playing away to Wigan in the Premiership. With just ten minutes to go, Arsenal were cruising to victory with a 2–0 lead. Surely nothing could stop the Gunners from notching up yet another victory. But goals in the 80th and 89th minutes allowed Wigan to draw level to force an impressive draw. But the northerners weren't finished, and in the 90th minute Charles N'Zogbia fired in the goal that gave them (what had looked like) a highly improbable 3–2 victory.

You'd have thought that that was the greatest comeback of all time but I suggest you'd be wrong!

For the really 'greatest comeback' we have to go all the way back to 1957 and a League match between Charlton Athletic (at home) and Huddersfield Town.

At half-time Huddersfield were 2–0 up. In the second half things went even worse for Charlton, who had been playing with 10 men since the 20th minute (a player had gone off injured and there were no substitutes in those days): after 70 minutes they were 5–1 down. You wouldn't fancy their chances. However, Charlton scored a couple of goals, and it was suddenly 'game on' as both teams seemed to stop defending and go on the attack instead. With minutes to go, Charlton took the lead 6–5, but Huddersfield scored again and, with only four minutes remaining on the clock, the scoreline stood at 6–6. Then,

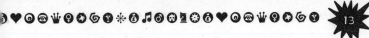

just as the referee was about to blow for full time, Charlton scored the winner. They had gone from 5–1 down to 7–6 winners in the space of 20 minutes. If only one could have been there . . . but, of course, many of the (home) fans left after 70 minutes – not wanting to see their side take any more punishment. Bet they never left a game early again!

Incidentally, Huddersfield Town are the only team to score six goals in a League match and still lose.

Essential Olympics

The ancient Olympic Games started in 776 BC. The very first Olympic race, held in 776 BC, was won by Corubus, a chef. Corubus – like all the runners in the race – would have been competing naked.

This race – a sprint of 192 metres (the length of the stadium) – was the only event in the first Olympics. The next race (over 400 metres) wasn't added till 50 years later. The other events – like the pentathlon, the wrestling and the boxing – were added even later – though by today's standards there still weren't many events.

The winners were presented with olive wreaths or crowns, but not medals.

The games were held every four years, and a four-year period was known as an Olympiad. The ceremonies included ritual sacrifices honouring the gods.

Only free men who spoke Greek could compete in the Games, which were held until AD 393, when they were suppressed by Theodosius I as part of his campaign to impose Christianity as a state religion – though why he found the Games incompatible with Christianity is a mystery. Interestingly, there is now some archaeological evidence to suggest that smaller versions of the Games might have continued unofficially for a while.

The brainchild of Baron Pierre de Coubertin, the first modern Olympic Games were held in Athens, Greece, in 1896. There were 311 male competitors but no female ones.

Great Britain was one of just 14 teams to compete in the 1896 Summer Olympics.

In 1896 only first- and second-place finishers of the events were awarded medals. The winners received silver medals and crowns of olive branches, while second-place finishers were given bronze medals.

The official Olympic flag, with its five interconnected rings on a white background, was created by Baron Pierre de Coubertin in 1914, and was first flown during the 1920 Olympic Games. The five rings symbolize the five main continents and are interconnected to demonstrate the friendship that the Games should bring to countries and competitors alike. The colours – blue, yellow, black, green and red – were chosen because at least one of them appeared on the flag of every country in the world.

Baron Pierre de Coubertin also chose the Olympic motto, *Citius, Altius, Fortius*

('Swifter, Higher, Stronger'), and wrote an Olympic oath for the athletes to recite at each Olympic Games. The Olympic oath states: 'In the name of all competitors, I promise that we shall take part in these Olympic Games, respecting and abiding by the rules that govern them, in the true spirit of sportsmanship, for the glory of sport and the honour of our teams.' During the opening ceremonies, one athlete recites the oath on behalf of all the athletes. The Olympic oath was first taken during the 1920 Olympic Games by Belgian fencer (and swimmer) Victor Boin.

And then there's the Olympic creed – which is meant to symbolize the ethos or spirit of the Games. The Olympic creed states: 'The most important thing in the Olympic Games is not to win but to take part, just as the most important thing in life is not the triumph but the struggle. The essential thing is not to have conquered but to have fought well.'

The lighting of the Olympic flame was derived from the ancient Olympic Games. In Olympia (Greece) a flame was ignited by the sun and then kept burning until the closing of the Games. In the modern era the flame first appeared at the 1928 Olympic Games in Amsterdam. Later, it became a relay, with the torch passed from runner to runner from the ancient site of Olympia to the stadium in the hosting city. The flame is then kept alight until the Games have finished.

The Olympic Brolly

The honour of hosting the Games is always awarded to a city and not to a country.

The Olympic Torch

Because of the outbreak of major world wars, there were no Olympic Games in 1916, 1940 and 1944. The 1916 Games would have been held in Berlin; 1940 would have been Tokyo but they pulled out, to be replaced by Helsinki (though, in the event, they didn't take place there either); 1944 would have been London – it didn't happen, and so London hosted the Games in 1948 instead.

Germany, Austria, Bulgaria, Hungary and Turkey were not invited to the 1920 Games as they were on the wrong (i.e. losing) side in the First World War. Germany was still banned in 1924, but the other four countries were allowed back in.

The Olympic medals are designed specially for each individual Olympic Games by the host city's organizing committee. Each medal must be at least 3mm thick and 60mm in diameter. Also, the gold and silver Olympic medals must be made out of 92.5 per cent silver, with the gold medal covered in six grams of gold.

A lot of attention is paid to the opening ceremony of the Games and it's usually an

elaborate affair. During the ceremony there is a procession of every country's athletes in alphabetical order – except for the last team, which is always the team representing the host nation.

The 1924 Games were originally destined for Amsterdam, but they were moved to Paris at the urging of Baron de Coubertin. He was about to retire and wanted to see them in his homeland one last time.

About 50,000 volunteers are involved in staging the Olympic Games.

The first Winter Olympic Games were held in 1908 – the same year as the Summer Olympic Games. This continued until 1992, when it was decided to stagger the two events. So the Winter Games were held in 1994 instead.

Until the 1970s, only amateurs were allowed to compete in the Olympics. Today, professionals can compete in any sport except boxing.

The 2016 Games will be held in Rio de Janeiro, Brazil.

Firsts

The first English Football League game to be broadcast live on the radio was Arsenal versus Sheffield United in 1927. To help listeners visualize the action, the BBC employed a grid system, published in the *Radio Times*, which divided the pitch into squares. And that's how we get the saying 'Back to square one', as the presenter would be directing the listener to where the ball had been placed.

Coincidentally, the Gunners were also involved in the first live coverage of a soccer match on television. In 1937 an exhibition match between Arsenal's first team and their reserves was televised live.

In 1889 Rotherham United goalkeeper Arthur Wharton, who was born in Ghana, became Britain's first black professional footballer.

The first pair of twins to score in the same League match were Bill and Alf Stephens, who scored both of Swindon's goals in a 2–0 victory over Exeter City in 1946–47.

The first female jockey to ride in the Grand National was Charlotte Brew in 1977 on Barony Fort (which refused at the fourth fence from home). In 1982 Geraldine Rees became the first female jockey to complete the race when she finished eighth on Cheers. The race awaits its first female winner – although Jenny Pitman has had successes as a trainer with Corbiere (1983) and Royal Athlete (1995).

In 2003–04 Arsenal became the first club to win the Premiership without losing a single game.

In 2010 Spain became the first European country to win a football World Cup held outside Europe. The final – in which Spain beat Holland – was also the first final between two monarchies.

The first marathon was run in 490 BC by Pheidippides, a Greek soldier, who ran from Marathon to Athens (about 25 miles) to tell the Athenians about the battle between the Greeks and the invading Persians. Poor old Pheidippides arrived in Athens exhausted and with bleeding feet. After telling the townspeople of the Greeks' success, he promptly fell down dead. In 1896, at the first modern Olympic Games, it was decided to hold a race of approximately the same distance in honour of Pheidippides' marathon run. One question, though: since the run was from Marathon to Athens, why was it called a marathon and not an athens? Just a thought.

The 2006 FIFA World Cup was the first where the first and last goals of the tournament were scored by defenders.

The first time a boxer won the world heavyweight championship from the canvas (i.e. the floor) was in 1930, when Germany's Max Schmeling was awarded the fight because of a low blow (i.e. one below the belt) from Jack Sharkey.

The first international cricket match took place in 1844 and was held between the US and Canada in New York. Canada won by 23 runs.

The first international Test match took place in 1877 and *did* involve Australia and England! Played in Melbourne, it finished with Australia winning by 45 runs. 100 years later, in 1977, a centenary Test match between the

two countries was played in Melbourne. Bet you can't guess the result . . . yup, Australia beat England by 45 runs – the margin by which they had won the inaugural match 100 years earlier.

Going back to that first Test in 1877, Australia's Charles Bannerman set a number of records. He faced the first ball in Test cricket, scored the first run, the first four and the first century. He ended up scoring 165 not out in Australia's total of 245 all out – his innings constituting over two-thirds (67.34 per cent) of the team's total. Incredibly, this is still the highest percentage scored by a batsman in a completed Test innings.

Incidentally, Charles Bannerman also went on to become the first Australian to score a century in England (though it wasn't in a Test match).

But that's not all! The first radio broadcast of a cricket match anywhere in the world was a 1922–23 match played as a benefit for Charles Bannerman, from which he received £490.

The first FA Cup final to feature numbered shirts was in 1933.

The first football World Cup finals to feature numbered shirts took place in 1938.

England footballers first wore their names on the backs of their shirts during the 1992 European Championships.

In tennis, the Grand Slam is achieved by winning the singles championships at the French Open, Wimbledon, the US Open and the Australian Open in the same calendar year. The first man to manage this feat was the American Don Budge in 1938; the first woman was the American Maureen Connolly in 1953. Since then, only Rod Laver (1962 and 1969), Margaret Court (1970) and Steffi Graf (1988) have done so.

As you might know, when cricket first started, bowlers used to bowl the ball underarm. In fact, overarm bowling was actually illegal. It was introduced to cricket by a Kent cricketer, John Willes, who picked it up from his sister, Christina Willes. She was bowling to him in a practice game, but when she found her skirt was getting in the way of her bowling underarm, she tried overarm instead!

Willes wasn't much of a cricketer (in just five

first-class matches between 1806 and 1822, he scored nine runs and took six wickets), but he is credited with being the first man to bowl overarm. In truth, there had been such bowlers in the 18th century, but they had been banned. So all Willes really did was revive a lost art. At first umpires tolerated it, but as more players adopted the style, it became officially accepted and legalized in 1835 – 13 years after Willes had retired.

The first British club to enter the European Cup was Hibernian in 1955.

Although men had worn shorts at Wimbledon since 1930, in 1933 the British tennis player Bunny Austin became the first man to wear shorts (albeit very long shorts!) on Wimbledon's historic Centre Court.

In golf, the word 'par' means the target or regulation number of shots for a hole or for a course. So the typical hole is either par 3, par 4 or par 5, while par for most golf courses ranges from 70 to 72. Par was first adopted in 1912.

Inspired by the marathon in the first modern Olympics the year before, the first Boston Marathon took place in 1897. There were just 15 runners, and of these, only 10 actually completed the race.

In football, the two-handed throw-in was first made compulsory in 1883, while goal nets

were first used in 1891. In the same year, the penalty kick was introduced into the game. The first ever penalty kick was awarded to Wolverhampton Wanderers in their game against Accrington Stanley on 14 September 1891. The penalty was taken and scored by a man named John Heath.

In the US, the first outdoor miniature golf courses were built on rooftops in New York City in 1926.

In 1895 the Derby became the first horse race to be filmed. It was also the first horse race to be televised (in 1932).

David Beckham played his first Premier League game not for Manchester United but for Preston North End – against Doncaster Rovers in 1995. On loan from United, Beckham appeared as a second-half substitute and scored in a 2–2 draw. He made his full Premier League debut in Preston's following match at home to Fulham, and scored again in a 3–2 win.

Which was the first football club to add 'City' to their title? Manchester? Leicester? Birmingham? Keep on guessing! In fact, it was Lincoln in 1892.

The first FA Cup final to go to extra time was the 1875 game between the Royal Engineers and the Old Etonians. However, even after 120 minutes the two teams couldn't be separated and the match finished 1–1. Three days later, the Engineers won the replay 2–0 – not least because some of the Old Etonian team couldn't make the game because of other commitments!

Cricket was the first sport to enclose its venues and charge for admission. The first time this happened was in 1731, when the

playing area on Kennington Common was staked out and roped off – thus enabling those running the game to charge people to watch it.

Croquet was the first sport to embrace equality, with both sexes allowed to play the game on an equal footing.

The first sport to be filmed was boxing in 1894.

The first Australian cricket tour of England took place in 1868. The touring party was made up entirely of aborigines (native Australians), and the players wore caps of different colours so that the spectators could identify them. The Australians played 47 matches against various teams, of which they won 14, lost 14 and drew the rest. Apart from playing cricket, the aborigines demonstrated a number of unique sports, including boomerang throwing, the backwards race, and cricket-ball dodging.

The first Paralympic Games were held in 1948. People – mistakenly – think that the world 'Paralympic' is derived from the words 'Paralysed' and 'Olympics'. In fact, that's only half right: it comes from the words 'Parallel' and 'Olympics' (i.e. the Paralympics are held in parallel with the Olympics).

The very first cricket World Cup was held in England in 1975.

The first cricket World Cup to feature an African Test nation (South Africa) was in 1992.

The first football team to wear shin guards was Nottingham Forest in 1874. They were invented by the centre forward, Sam Widdowson, who wore them outside his socks.

The first woman to play golf at St Andrew's Golf Club in Scotland was Mary, Queen of Scots, in 1552. She was the club's founder.

The first team to remain undefeated throughout the whole cricket World Cup was Australia in 2003. They repeated this feat in the 2007 tournament.

In 1901 Tottenham Hotspur – then not even in the Football League – won the FA Cup and, at the celebration dinner, became the first club to tie (blue and white) ribbons to the handles of the trophy, a practice which has since become a custom.

In 2006 Switzerland became the first team to be eliminated from the football World Cup finals without conceding a goal.

Lasts

The last Olympics in which the gold medals were made entirely of gold were in 1912.

The last time a First Division or Premiership club had two players scoring more than 30 goals in a season was Sunderland in 1935–36, when Raich Carter and Bob Gurney each scored 31 goals.

Eight-ball overs were last used at Test level in 1978–79 in Australia and New Zealand.

In 1932–33 Dennis Smith of New Zealand dismissed Eddie Paynter of England with his very first ball in Test cricket. Unfortunately for Dennis, it wasn't just his first wicket in Test cricket but also his last as he never took another!

Every year the football teams of England, Scotland, Wales and Northern Ireland competed for the British Championship. The last one was in the 1983–84 season, and Northern Ireland won – for only the third time in their history – and so kept the trophy.

Oops!

When Celestine Babayaro made his debut for Chelsea in a pre-season match, he was thrilled to score – so thrilled that he broke his leg while celebrating, putting him out of action for much of the season.

English referee Graham Poll mistakenly handed out *three* yellow cards to Croatia's Josip Šimuni in a 2006 football World Cup match against Australia.

The great South African golfer Gary Player was once accused of being lucky. 'That's funny,' he replied. 'The harder I practise, the luckier I get.' Fabulous response, but obviously he could have used a bit more practice in a 1955 tournament in Huddersfield, England. At the final hole he was in the lead and needed just a par four to win. His second shot landed near the green, a few inches from a stone wall. Because there

was no room for a backswing and Player
didn't want to waste a stroke knocking the
ball clear of the wall, he decided to make
the ball ricochet off the wall. It didn't work
out exactly the way he planned. The ball
bounced back and hit him in the face. Player
was not only hurt but was also penalized two
strokes for 'impeding the flight of the ball' –
and duly lost the tournament. All together
now . . . oops!

When the Italian striker Giuseppe Meazza took a penalty in the semi-final of the 1938 World Cup, his shorts fell down.

Brazilian soccer star Ronaldinho was filming a TV commercial when he fluffed an overhead kick and smashed the stained-glass window of a 12th-century cathedral.

Every year some 20 million golf balls are lost in water hazards on British golf courses.

In the 1950 football World Cup the USA beat England 1–0. Many British newspapers couldn't believe the scoreline and so printed the result as 10–1 to England.

The 1908 Olympic marathon was a bit of a shambles. The Italian Dorando Pietri was so exhausted, he had to be helped across the finishing line. Although he was initially declared the winner, he was later disqualified in favour of Johnny Hayes of the US.

Mind you, this was nothing compared to the 1904 marathon. The American runner Fred Lorz dropped out after nine miles and was given a lift back to the stadium by his manager. When he was seen trotting over the finish line (to retrieve his clothes), the officials thought he had won the race. Lorz played along with it until he was found out shortly after the medal ceremony. He was banned for a year.

But that wasn't the only extraordinary occurrence in the race. A Cuban postman named Félix Carbajal decided to join in –

running in ordinary trousers that he cut off at the knee to make them look like shorts. On the way, he stopped off in an orchard and ate some apples for a snack. Alas, they turned out to be rotten and made him ill, forcing him to lie down and take a nap. Despite all this, he finished in fourth place.

Meanwhile Thomas Hicks of the US was the first to cross the finish-line legally – but only after receiving several doses of strychnine sulphate mixed with brandy from his trainers, who also physically helped him to cross the finishing line. In fact, Hicks was in such a bad state that he had to be carried off the track and might very well have died in the stadium had he not received treatment from several doctors. Still, he was awarded the gold medal.

As you know, no bowler can bowl two consecutive overs, but in a 1951 Test against England, Alex Moir of New Zealand did just that. He bowled the last over before the tea break and the first over afterwards. Silly umpires for not spotting that one!

At a football match in 2009 the officials of

Bishop Auckland FC held a minute's silence for one of their former players. Nothing wrong with that, you might think . . . except the player being honoured was *still alive*!

Tommy Farrer, 86, was part of the Bishop Auckland team that had reached the FA Amateur Cup at Wembley three times. He also won 20 amateur international caps for England and played in the 1956 Olympics in Melbourne.

The club printed tributes to him in their programme and in the local paper, but discovered their mistake when they rang his wife to offer their sympathy – and was told he had just popped out to the shops.

Tommy said, 'I think it's hilarious. And it's quite nice actually – there's not many people who get to know what sort of tribute they'll receive.'

In the 1956 Grand National, the jockey Dick Francis was in the lead just yards from the finishing line when his horse, Devon Loch, 'spooked' and unseated him. It was an extraordinarily unlucky thing to happen – not least for the Queen's mother, who owned

Devon Loch. Dick Francis went on to become a bestselling novelist.

The first League football match to be played under floodlights was between Portsmouth and Newcastle on 22 February 1956. The game was held up for 30 minutes when the fuses failed.

One of the most unusual injuries in the history of the football World Cup occurred in the very first tournament in 1930. In the semi-final between the US and Argentina, the American trainer ran onto the pitch to attend to an injured player and dropped his medicine box, breaking a bottle of chloroform. He inhaled the fumes, fell to the ground and had to be stretchered off the field. The injured player recovered without any treatment.

Soccer fanzines

Most British football clubs have 'fanzines' – magazines produced by fans. The longest-running fanzine is the *City Gent*, produced by supporters of Bradford City FC, which first went on sale at Valley Parade in November 1984 and has sold in excess of 300,000 copies. These used to be printed but nowadays many of them can be found online.

What I love about fanzines is that they're *by* the fans, *for* the fans, and they reflect what true fans really feel. This is reflected in the brilliant titles. The ones below aren't all necessarily still out there, but the memories – good and bad – will linger on for many years to come. I've given explanations (in brackets) for some of the titles . . . others, I'll leave to your imagination!

Linesman You're Rubbish – Aberystwyth Town
Shots in the Dark – Aldershot
The Gooner – Arsenal
Heroes & Villains – Aston Villa
The Ugly Duckling – Aylesbury United
(Aylesbury is famous for its ducks)

Revenge of the Killer Penguin – Bath City
Tired and Weary – Birmingham City
Our Flag's Been to Wembley – Braintree Town
(a great title that sums up the spirit of fans of
– shall we say – 'less successful' teams)
Beesotted – Brentford (Brentford are known
as the Bees)
Super Dario Land – Crewe Alexandra (the
Crewe manager, Dario Gradi, was the
Football League's longest-serving manager)
Mission Impossible – Darlington
Light at the End of the Tunnel – Dartford
(the Dartford Tunnel runs underneath the
Thames)
The Gibbering Clairvoyant – Dumbarton
It's Half Past Four . . . and We're 2–0 Down –
Dundee
We'll Score Again! – Exeter City
Crying Time Again – Hamilton Academicals
Monkey Business – Hartlepool Town (during
the Napoleonic wars of the early 19th
century, a French ship was wrecked off the
coast of Hartlepool. The only survivor was
a monkey which, as the ship's mascot, was
dressed in a uniform. On finding it, the locals
decided to hold a trial on the beach. Since
the monkey couldn't answer their questions –

A FRENCH SPY?.. MOI ?

and being unaware of what a Frenchman might look like – they decided that it was in fact a French spy and sentenced it to death. The poor creature was hanged from the mast of a fishing boat. For years, Hartlepool Town fans were teased about this by opposing fans, but now they've embraced their past: in fact their mascot is called H'Angus the Monkey)

Still Mustn't Grumble – Hearts

To Elland Back – Leeds United (Leeds play their home matches at Elland Road)

Where's the Money Gone? – Leicester City

Deranged Ferret – Lincoln City

Another Wasted Corner – Liverpool

Mad as a Hatter – Luton Town (the club are known as the Hatters because of the town's historical connection with the hat-making industry)

Mr Bismarck's Electric Pickelhaube – Meadowbank Thistle (great title but I have

absolutely *no* idea what it refers to!)

No One Likes Us – Millwall

Once Upon a Tyne – Newcastle United (the city of Newcastle is located on the River Tyne)

What a Load of Cobblers – Northampton Town (Northampton has always been famous for its shoemakers, who are also known as cobblers)

Get a Grip, Ref! – Scunthorpe United

Just Another Wednesday – Sheffield Wednesday

It's the Hope I Can't Stand! – Sunderland (a sentiment with which *every* soccer fan can sympathize. This actually comes from a line in the film *Clockwise*: John Cleese, playing a headmaster who has to get to a conference on time, says to his companion, 'It's not the despair, Laura. I can take the despair. It's the hope I can't stand!')

Flippin' Heck Ref, That Was a Foul Surely! – Waterlooville

Winning Isn't Everything – Welling United

The Sheeping Giant – Wrexham (there are a lot of sheep farms in the countryside near Wrexham)

Wimbledon

Wimbledon was the world's very first tennis tournament.

200 spectators turned up to watch the first championship in 1877, paying one shilling each. The first champion, Spencer Gore, won 12 guineas.

Even though no British man has won the men's singles since Fred Perry in 1936, the UK still holds the record – 35 – for the most wins.

It is Europe's largest single annual sporting catering operation. Some 1,600 catering staff will be on duty there.

More than 42,000 balls are used at the Wimbledon tennis tournament each year.

The first televised coverage of a Wimbledon match was in 1937.

Every morning of the fortnight, one hour before the gates open, Hamish the hawk is released to ward off the local pigeons.

In 1985 17-year-old Boris Becker of Germany became the youngest player, the first unseeded player and the first German to win the men's singles title.

Since 1949, singles champions have received miniature versions of the trophies.

Roger Federer (1998), Pat Cash (1982), Ivan Lendl (1978) and Bjorn Borg (1972) all won boys' singles titles.

There are more than 50,000 shrubs and

plants in the All England Club grounds.

Jimmy Connors was seeded in the singles championships a record 17 times between 1973 and 1989.

There are 375 full members of the All England Lawn Tennis and Croquet Club, plus a number of honorary members, including past singles champions.

The crowds consume 17,000 bottles of champagne, 300,000 cups of tea and coffee, and 250,000 bottles of water during the fortnight.

Full seeding (designed to ensure that the best players don't meet and knock each other out in the early stages of the tournament) began in 1927.

Since 2003 the only members of the royal family to whom players leaving the court have had to bow or curtsey are the Queen and the Prince of Wales.

Martina Navratilova holds the record for the most matches played by a woman (326).

Jean Borotra holds the record for the most

matches played by a man (223). In 1964 he took part in the men's doubles at the age of 65.

Chairs were first provided for players to sit on between changing ends in 1975.

In 1952 Frank Sedgman became the first man to be seeded top in all three events (men's singles, men's doubles and mixed doubles).

The yellow tennis balls, which were first used in 1986, are stored at 20 degrees Celsius.

The last ten british wimbledon singles champions:

Virginia Wade 1977
Ann Jones 1969
Angela Mortimer 1961
Dorothy Round 1937
Fred Perry 1936
Kitty Godfree 1926
Dorothea Lambert Chambers 1914
Ethel Larcombe 1912
Arthur W. Gore 1909
Dora Boothby 1909

The Olympick Games and the Olympian Games

No, this isn't a misprint but an intriguing tale of what a single man can do if he really puts his mind to it.

As you know, when it comes to the Olympics, there was a bit of a gap between the end of the ancient Olympics (AD 393) and the start of the modern Olympics (1896). You might have assumed that there was nothing in between the two, but you'd have been wrong! For let me introduce you to a 17th-century English lawyer named Robert Dover who, in 1612, started the 'Olympick Games upon the Cotswold Hills' in Chipping Campden.

These games, held in the early summer, were presided over by Mr Dover on his horse. Competitors were summoned to the hill by the sounding of a hunting horn, and the games themselves were started by the firing of a cannon. They consisted of swordplay, cudgel-play (fighting with a large club),

sledgehammer-throwing and chess. There were lots of spectators: the gentry were provided with tents and commoners were given rugs to sit on.

The English Civil War (between the Roundheads and the Cavaliers) brought the games to an end in 1652. After the restoration of the King (Charles II) in 1660, the games were reintroduced on a smaller scale, but they were never the same without Robert Dover, who had died.

The Cotswold games were started up again in the 1960s, on the same site (now called Dover Hill), and soon attracted thousands of visitors.

So much for the Olympicks . . . now let me tell you about the Olympian Games or, to be more accurate, Brookes's 'Olympian Games', as started by Dr William Penny Brookes of Much Wenlock in Shropshire in 1850.

These games were much more extensive than Mr Dover's and included football, cricket, running and long jump. There was also pig racing and a blind wheelbarrow race. I have to say I'd pay good money to watch pigs racing. The prizes included cash, medals and a laurel-wreath crown.

Buoyed by his success, five years later, in 1865, Brookes founded the National (British) Olympic Association, which held its first games at London's famous Crystal Palace. Alas, he couldn't get sponsorship and so was unable to attract the leading sportsmen of the day. However, he persevered with his Much Wenlock games, and these were brought to the attention of one Baron Coubertin, who wrote to Brookes in 1889. The following year the baron visited Much Wenlock to watch the games for himself.

It was this experience – perhaps more than any other – that persuaded the baron to set up a modern international Olympic Games, and in 1894 he founded the International Olympic Committee (IOC), with the first modern Olympics taking place in Athens just two years later.

Alas, Dr Brookes died just months before the Games at the age of 86. However, his influence lives on – especially in his idea of holding the Games at different venues rather than at one permanent site.

Confirmation of Dr Brookes's importance

came in 1994 – a full 100 years after the establishment of the IOC – when the head of the committee, Juan Antonio Samaranch, paid a visit to Much Wenlock, where he laid a wreath on Brookes's grave. He gave a speech in which he said, 'I came to pay homage and tribute to Dr Brookes, who really was the founder of the modern Olympic Games.'

Robert Dover and William Brookes: two men with one vision; two men ahead of their time.

Expressions we get from baseball

Ballpark figure – approximate number

Cover all the bases — ensure safety

Curveball – a surprise

Double header – two contests/events held on the same day

Playing hardball (as in 'he's playing hardball with us') – as opposed to softball

Heavy hitter — a powerful person

Home run — a total success (opposite of strike out)

Left field (as in 'that idea came out of left field') – unusual or unexpected

The majors (as in 'to be playing in the majors') – at the top, in the big or major league

Play ball — go along with something; start

Rain check (as in 'to take a rain check') — do something at a later date

Step up to the plate – to rise to the occasion

Three strikes and you're out – you get two chances before you're held to account

Touch base (as in 'let's touch base later') – to talk later, to see that all is well

Whole new ball game – an altered situation

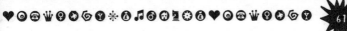

All the football clubs to have finished runners-up without ever winning the Premier League (or old First Division) title

Bristol City (1906–07)

Oldham Athletic (1914–15)

Cardiff City (1923–24)

Leicester City (1928–29)

Charlton Athletic (1936–37)

Blackpool (1955–56)

Queens Park Rangers (1975–76)

Watford (1982–83)

Southampton (1983–84)

Cross-Channel swimming

Captain Matthew Webb (1848–1883) became
the first person to swim the English Channel
when, on 25 August 1875, he crossed from
Dover to Calais. It took him just under 22
hours.

It wasn't until 1923 – 48 years later – that
Enrico Tiraboschi made the first crossing of
the English Channel from France to England.

Some of the more extraordinary
cross-channel swims and swimmers:

As of 2010, Alison Streeter has swum the

Channel 43 times. Her fastest time is just under nine hours. She is the first (and so far only) woman to swim the Channel three ways non-stop. Think about that for a second. Three ways non-stop . . . That means she swam the Channel, then swam back, and then, when any other person would be totally exhausted, swam it again. The three crossings (in 1990) took 34 hours and 40 minutes.

Only two men have achieved that feat – one slower (Jon Erikson in 1981 in a time of 38 hours and 27 minutes) and one faster (Philip Rush in 1987 in a time of 28 hours and 21 minutes).

I'm a good swimmer and regularly swim a

kilometre (in a heated swimming pool), but the thought of 21 miles (33 kilometres) in rough seas is crazy. As for doing it three times in succession . . .

Interestingly, this is clearly one area where women compete on equal terms with men. Indeed, Alison Streeter's closest rival – Kevin Murphy – has swum the Channel fewer times than Alison: 34 (including three double-Channel swims). But even so, what a great man!

The fastest swim across the Channel (by a man) was six hours 57 minutes (this was the Bulgarian Petar Stoychev in 2007), while the fastest swim (by a woman) was seven hours 25 minutes (Yvetta Hlavacova of the Czech Republic).

The oldest person to swim the Channel was the 70-year-old American George Brunstad; the youngest was Thomas Gregory, a British boy of just under 12. The youngest girl – Samantha Druce, also British – was just over 12.

However, the most famous cross-Channel swimmer is probably the comedian David

Walliams, who astonished the world when he completed the crossing in the very fast time of 10 hours and 34 minutes. It was undertaken in 2006 for Sport Relief, and he raised over £1 million in donations.

But what of brave Captain Webb, the pioneer of cross-Channel swimming? He retained his passion for dangerous swims, and in 1883 he decided to swim through the Whirlpool Rapids below Niagara Falls. Alas, it was a feat too far and he drowned. In 1909 Webb's brother Thomas unveiled a memorial in Dawley, Shropshire, which bore the inscription: NOTHING GREAT IS EASY.

Celebrities and sport

Soccer

Singer Rod Stewart (had a trial for Brentford)

Chef Gordon Ramsay (played twice for Rangers)

Boxer Audley Harrison (had a trial for Watford)

Tennis player Andy Murray (had a trial for Rangers)

TV presenter Sir David Frost (had a trial for Nottingham Forest)

Rock star Gavin Rossdale (had a trial for Chelsea)

Westlife singer Nicky Byrne (had a trial for Leeds United as a goalkeeper but was too short)

Actor Josh Hartnett (only turned to acting after his soccer career ended)

Men whose fathers were professional footballers

Comedian Alan Carr (for Northampton Town)

Actor Jimmy Nail (for Huddersfield Town)

Actor Colin Farrell (for Shamrock Rovers – and his uncle too)

TV presenter Les Dennis (for Liverpool)

Boxer Ricky Hatton (for Manchester City)

Actor Ian McShane (for Manchester United)

Rowing

House star Hugh Laurie won a Blue for rowing in the Boat Race for Cambridge against Oxford.

Polo

Model Jodie Kidd is a top polo player who was chosen to represent England in the 2003 World Polo Championships.

Actor Tommy Lee Jones is a champion polo player.

Tennis

Rugby legend J. P. R. Williams won Junior Wimbledon and could have played tennis for a career if he hadn't decided to become a doctor and play rugby for Wales and the British Lions.

Actor Matthew Perry was ranked number two at tennis in Ottawa at the age of 13.

Actress Joely Richardson attended a Florida tennis academy for two years.

Cricket

TV presenter Michael Parkinson was a talented cricketer, playing for Barnsley (with Dickie Bird and Geoffrey Boycott) and being given a trial for Yorkshire CCC.

Ex-footballer and TV presenter Gary Lineker played second XI cricket for Leicestershire and once scored a century for the MCC playing at Lord's.

Sherlock Holmes author Sir Arthur Conan Doyle was a keen amateur cricketer who bowled out the great W. G. Grace in 1900.

Gymnastics

TV presenter Gabby Logan represented Wales at gymnastics in the 1990 Commonwealth Games.

Actress Jennifer Lopez was a star gymnast at high school.

Actor Sir David Jason won prizes for gymnastics at school.

Motor racing

The late Oscar-winning actor Paul Newman once achieved second place in the gruelling 24-hour Le Mans race.

Athletics

Singer/songwriter Sheryl Crow was a competitive hurdler.

Ex-Spice Girl Mel C ran for the county of Cheshire when she was a schoolgirl.

Weightlifting

Ex-actor – and former Governor of California

– Arnold Schwarzenegger was not only a bodybuilding champion but also won the Austrian Junior Olympic Weightlifting Championship.

Boxing

Rap star 50 Cent was a talented boxer who thought about becoming a professional.

Actor Robert De Niro learned to box for his Oscar-winning role as Jake La Motta in *Raging Bull* and was so good that La Motta himself said that he could have taken it up professionally.

Actor Mickey Rourke had 26 amateur fights in the 1970s, and then quit when his acting career took off. In recent years he has returned to the ring with some success. Ironically, his Oscar nomination came for playing the title role in *The Wrestler*!

Actor Liam Neeson boxed for a local team from the age of nine until 17 (in one early match his nose was broken and he had it set on the spot by his manager).

American Football

Actor and comedian Bill Cosby was good enough to be offered a trial with the Green Bay Packers.

Actor Warren Beatty was offered scholarships as an American football player from several universities but turned them all down to concentrate on acting.

Baseball

Actor William Baldwin was talented enough to have originally considered a professional career with the New York Yankees.

Actor Billy Crystal attended college on a full baseball scholarship but decided not to pursue a career in the sport.

Actor George Clooney once tried out for the Cincinnati Reds baseball team.

Wrestling

When he was starting out, actor Kirk Douglas supplemented his meagre earnings with professional appearances in the ring.

Actor Tom Cruise was an all-round sporting star at school but he turned to acting after injuring his knee wrestling.

Figure Skating

Actress Sarah Michelle Gellar was a competitive figure skater for three years and, at her peak, was ranked third in New York State.

Swimming

TV presenter, artist and singer Rolf Harris was

Junior Backstroke Champion of all Australia in 1946.

Actress Hilary Swank swam in the Junior Olympics; she was also a top gymnast.

Actor James Alexandrou swam for his county and was ranked in the national Top 10.

Golf
Actress Ellen DeGeneres considered becoming a professional.

Basketball
Actress Queen Latifah was a power forward on two state championship basketball teams in high school.

Ice Hockey
Late actor Heath Ledger nearly became a professional ice-hockey player but chose acting over sport.

Actor Keanu Reeves was the goalkeeper in his high school ice-hockey team, where he earned the nickname 'The Wall' and was voted MVP (Most Valuable Player).

Volleyball
Brazilian supermodel Gisele Bündchen originally wanted to be a professional volleyball player.

Snooker
Actor Darren Day was a semi-professional snooker player.

Equestrianism
Actress Kate Bosworth was a champion equestrian; she also played soccer and lacrosse.

TV presenter Jonathan Dimbleby was Showjumping Champion of the South of England in 1964.

Squash
Actor Martin Freeman was in the England junior squash squad.

Martial Arts
Actor Ryan Phillippe has a black belt in tae kwon do.

Motor-racing driver Lewis Hamilton gained his karate black belt at the age of 12.

Fencing
Ioan Gruffudd, Antonio Banderas, Sylvester Stallone, Elijah Wood, Keira Knightley, Madonna, Uma Thurman, James McAvoy.

Other celebrities and sport
Charlie Chaplin was a fine table-tennis player who thought he'd be able to beat Maxwell Woosnam, a champion, who was using a butter knife in place of a bat. Woosnam won, and then chucked Chaplin into his own swimming pool.

Famous winning owners of the Grand National include the Prince of Wales (later King Edward VII), whose horse Ambush II won in 1900, and the comedian Freddie Starr, whose horse Minnehoma was the 1994 winner.

When P Diddy became the first rap performer to be given a star on the Hollywood Walk of Fame, how do you think he celebrated? Well, you'd be wrong! He held a croquet party!

Olympic firsts

There must have been a first gold medallist at the first ever modern Olympics (1896) . . . so (hop) step (and jump) forward James B. Connolly of the US, the winner of the hop, step and jump (the event that we would now call the triple jump), which was the first of the finals in those games – making Connolly the first Olympic champion of the modern Olympics!

The first opening ceremony was held at the 1908 Olympic Games in London.

Women weren't allowed to compete in the first modern Olympics (which suggests that they weren't that 'modern'). They first competed at the 1900 Paris Games, where 11 women were allowed to take part in lawn tennis and golf.

The first woman to win an Olympic event was England's Charlotte Cooper, who won the tennis singles in 1900.

The 1912 Games were the first where women

were allowed to enter swimming events. However, there were no American participants as their Olympic committee didn't allow them to compete in events without wearing long skirts – a restriction that would have made swimming impossible . . .

It wasn't until 1928 that women were permitted to compete in track-and-field events for the first time. The longest distance they were allowed to run was 800 metres, but so many of the competitors collapsed at the end of the race that they were banned from running such distances until 1960. And to think that women now run marathons . . .

Women had to wait till 1984 before they could take part in shooting events, and not until 2000 were they allowed to compete in weightlifting.

Iranian women competed in the Olympics for the first time at the 1996 Games.

In 1900 football became the first team sport to be added to the Olympics.

Beach volleyball was first added to the Olympic Games in 1996.

The Winter Olympics were held for the first time in 1924 – in Chamonix, France.

Electric timing devices and a public address system were first used at the 1912 Olympics.

The first time that athletes marched into the stadium behind the flag of their country was in London in 1908.

Eleanor Holm was the first woman . . . Well, you read her story and you decide! Having won the 100m backstroke gold medal for the US in 1932, Holm had been unbeaten for seven years when she travelled to Germany for the 1936 Olympics in the expectation of retaining her title. The trouble started on the voyage over. After getting drunk at parties on board ship, she was expelled from the team. She still had a good time in Berlin – meeting Hermann Goering, who gave her a silver swastika: she had a mould made of it, into which she put a diamond (Jewish) star of David.

So was she the first woman expellee? Or, much better, the first female athlete to get one over on the Nazis?

It's your choice!

In 2000 Sir Steven Redgrave became the first
– and so far *only* – athlete to win gold medals
in five consecutive Olympics.

The 1956 Games were the first to be held in
the southern hemisphere. However, because
back then the Australians didn't allow horses
to be brought into the country, the equestrian
events took place in Stockholm, Sweden.

In 1968 Mexico City became the first Latin American venue for the Olympics. These were also the first Games to be held at an altitude above 2,000 metres (over 2,200 in fact). The thin air posed problems for athletes in endurance events, but it led to records in short races, relays and, especially, jumping events.

It was at these Games that Bob Beamon produced a jump that shattered the existing long-jump record and remained the world record for a staggering 23 years. It was also the Games where Dick Fosbury first revolutionized the high jump with his back-first 'Fosbury flop' technique – the one that every high jumper now uses – to win the gold medal.

In 1976 Nadia Comaneci of Romania became the first gymnast to achieve a perfect score of 10. The 14-year-old scored seven perfect 10s at the games – winning five medals (including three golds) in the process.

Unbelievable (1)

One of the pleasures of researching and writing these books is that I uncover some factual gems. It's a well-known fact that the record score for a British (professional) soccer match is Arbroath 36, Bon Accord 0. It's an amazing score, but what's *really* incredible about it is that *on the very same day and in the very same competition* – 12 September 1885, the Scottish Cup – Dundee Harp beat Aberdeen Rovers 35–0.

So picture the scene. You're one of the Dundee Harp team celebrating your record victory when you discover that another side has gone one better. In fact, it was the Dundee Harp captain – a former Arbroath player – who got the news after he sent his former team a telegram to boast about the (he thought) record score. Truly unbelievable!

But the drama doesn't end there. According to the referee in the Dundee Harp v. Aberdeen Rovers game, the final score was 37–0, but the club secretary of Dundee Harp – the winning team, remember – reckoned

that it was only 35–0, so the ref went with the lower figure. Can't make any difference, the club secretary must have thought, it's still the record score.

Er, no!

There were five one-eyed men in the 1920 France–Scotland rugby union match. One of them was the remarkable prop Marcel-Frédéric Lubin-Lebrère who, in the First World War just a few years earlier, had lost an eye and also had 23 pieces of shrapnel removed from his body. He later became Mayor of Toulouse.

In the 1979 India v. Pakistan Test match at Bangalore, an invasion of bees halted play, prompting the players and umpires to lie face down and cover their ears.

The man who won the Indianapolis 500 in 1912 had to get out and push his stalled car for the last mile of the race.

Anne Ottenbrite of Canada won the 200m breaststroke in the Los Angeles Olympics in 1984, but only after a series of extraordinary bad luck. First, just before the Canadian trials to pick the team, she managed to dislocate her right kneecap while showing off a pair of shoes. Then, while in LA, she was involved in a car crash, and finally she managed to strain her thigh playing a computer game. Very bizarre!

In 2002 an American long-distance runner named Tom Johnson took on a leading endurance racehorse in a 50-mile race across the desert in the United Arab Emirates. Who would you have put your money on to win? Well, like me, you'd have lost because, incredibly, the man won – albeit by just 10 seconds in a race that took five hours and 45 minutes to complete. So how did he come to win? Well, he did have one big advantage as he was able to eat and drink while he ran. The horse, on the other hand, had to stop during the race to eat, drink and have a short rest.

Travelling at up to 120 miles per hour, a Formula One car generates so much downforce that, in theory, it could be driven upside down on the roof of a tunnel.

In 1979 England was playing Australia in Perth when the Australian Dennis Lillee was caught by Peter Willey off the bowling of Graham Dilley. So it was Lillee caught Willey bowled Dilley!

A semi-final wrestling bout in the 1912 Olympics lasted a staggering 11 hours! The winner, an Estonian named Martin Klein, was so exhausted that, understandably, he couldn't take part in the final the next day. Some victory, eh?

The Brazilian government couldn't afford to send its athletes to the 1932 Los Angeles Games, so they put them on a ship with

50,000 sacks of Brazilian coffee, which they sold at various ports along the way to pay for their expenses.

Today Test matches take place over five days. In the past, however, some Tests weren't subject to any time restrictions: they were played until their conclusion, regardless of how long that took. In 1939 England and South Africa played for 14 days straight in Durban, South Africa, in what became known as the Timeless Test. The remarkable thing about this marathon is that even after such a long time, it still wasn't finished! England needed 42 more runs to win, and had five wickets in hand, but the team's boat was due to sail home the next day, and so the game was called off.

Stanisława Walasiewicz – or Stella Walsh, as she was known in her adopted country of America – ran the 100 metres in 1932, and then competed again in 1936 for her native Poland, but only because the US couldn't support her financially. However, when the athlete was shot dead in Cleveland in 1980, the autopsy revealed that she was actually . . . a man!

Sheffield Wednesday didn't compete in the 1886–87 FA Cup – likewise Birmingham City in 1921–22 and Queens Park Rangers in 1926–27 – and all for the same reason: having completed their application forms for the Cup, office staff forgot to post them to the Football Association.

In 1958–59 the Gateshead United team contained two players whose name was Ken Smith. For identification purposes the Football League designated them Ken Smith 1 and Ken Smith 2. All very straightforward – until Gateshead beat Carlisle United, with Ken Smith 1 scoring twice and Ken Smith 2 scoring once. The result in the paper read: Gateshead 3 (K. Smith 1 (2), K. Smith 2 (1)).

That's interesting (2)

Sometimes I discover something that is so extraordinary that I have to share it with my readers – albeit with a warning that it might not be true. This is such a fact. In all first-class cricket there has never been a completed individual innings of precisely 228. Now, I have looked through hundreds of scorecards and, indeed, haven't found such a score – but that doesn't necessarily mean that it's true. So keep an eye out for a batsman being dismissed on 228 and, if you find one, do please post it on my webpage!

With one pitch, the great baseball player Babe Ruth could throw two balls simultaneously, and they would remain parallel all the way to the catcher.

Let me tell you about one of the strangest ever episodes in top-flight football. In 1996 Ali Dia – or Ali Dire, as he became known – was struggling to make a living in the lower reaches of French football. So he decided to try his luck in England. He was turned down by a couple of League clubs but he managed to sign semi-professional terms with non-league Blyth Spartans. This was probably just about his level, but Dia wanted more – so he launched an audacious bid to get into a Premiership club.

He got in touch with Southampton boss Graeme Souness, and (wrongly) claimed that he had 13 caps for Senegal and was related to Liberian superstar striker George Weah (he wasn't). However, a phone call from someone pretending to be Weah was enough to persuade the Saints to hand him a contract. Dia was lined up to play in a reserve game, but after that was cancelled, he was thrown straight in at the deep end with a place on the bench against Leeds. When the great Matt Le Tissier was injured after half an hour, there was huge excitement in the crowd as the new signing, the cousin of the great

George Weah, came onto the field.

It was truly awful. Dia was . . . well, *dire*, and was himself substituted.

It turned out that the man who had pretended to be George Weah on the other end of the phone had actually been Dia's agent. Southampton – obviously – cancelled his contract.

Still, you've got to admire his nerve!

The Olympic Games and how the UK performed

YEAR	VENUE	UK'S POSITION IN THE FINAL MEDAL TABLE
1896	Athens	5th
1900	Paris	3rd
1904	St Louis	6th
1908	London	1st
1912	Stockholm	3rd
1920	Antwerp	3rd
1924	Paris	4th
1928	Amsterdam	11th
1932	Los Angeles	8th
1936	Berlin	10th
1948	London	12th
1952	Helsinki	15th
1956	Melbourne	8th
1960	Rome	12th
1964	Tokyo	10th
1968	Mexico City	10th
1972	Munich	12th
1976	Montreal	13th
1980	Moscow	9th
1984	Los Angeles	11th
1988	Seoul	12th
1992	Barcelona	13th
1996	Atlanta	36th
2000	Sydney	10th
2004	Athens	10th
2008	Beijing	4th

That's interesting (3)

In 1905 18 men died from injuries sustained on the (American) football field. So President Theodore Roosevelt stepped in and insisted they make the game safer by outlawing foul play and brutality. In particular, he wanted the game's authorities to ban punching and gang tackling.

In football, a yo-yo club is one that's always getting promoted and then relegated again soon afterwards. According to statistics, Birmingham City have been promoted to and relegated from the top division more times than any other English club, with 12 promotions (1894, 1901, 1903, 1921, 1948, 1955, 1972, 1980, 1985, 2002, 2007 and 2009) and 11 relegations (1896, 1902, 1908, 1939, 1950, 1965, 1979, 1984, 1986, 2006 and 2008), including a run of four consecutive promotions/relegations from the 2005–06 season to the 2008–09 season.

Left-handed people are better at sports that require fast reactions and good spatial awareness.

James Gordon of Rangers was selected to play in all 11 positions, including goalkeeper, during his career at Ibrox Park from 1910 to 1930.

Until the 1870s baseball was played without the use of gloves.

Here's an odd thing . . . do you know which country won a soccer tournament for which they hadn't even qualified? Denmark initially failed to qualify for Euro 1992, finishing second in their qualifying group to Yugoslavia. However, because of the civil war taking place within its boundaries (the country itself would later be broken up into a number of different countries), Yugoslavia was expelled from the tournament and

Denmark took its place and went on to win
the whole tournament – beating Germany,
the reigning world champions, in the final. It
was Denmark's very first international trophy.

A cowboy in a rodeo bull-riding competition
must hang on for at least eight seconds for it
to count as a qualifying ride. Cowboys who
fail to stay on are eliminated until there's just
one cowboy left standing (er, just . . .).

After retiring from boxing, ex-world heavyweight champion Gene Tunney lectured on Shakespeare at Yale University.

Leyton Orient changed their name from Clapton Orient to Leyton Orient to just Orient, and then, in 1987, back to Leyton Orient again.

The 1904 Olympic Games – held in St Louis in the US – were a thoroughly American affair. Although there were representatives from 12 countries, 85 per cent (523) of the competitors were Americans, and eight per cent (52) were Canadians. The only other countries with more than 10 competitors were Germany (17) and Greece (14). There were only three Brits, two Australians and just one Frenchman.

At one stage in the 1920s Chelsea had three players who were medical students.

Racehorses have been known to wear out new shoes in just one race.

Golf was banned in England and Scotland in 1457 by King James II of Scotland because he claimed it distracted people from their archery practice.

English and Australian cricketers fear different scores. For Australians, the devil's number (or dreaded number) is a personal or team score of 87. Why? Because, according to Australian superstition, batsmen have a tendency to be dismissed for a score which is, of course, 13 (an unlucky number in many cultures) short of a century. The English equivalent is 111 (or a Nelson) – probably because the figure looks like three stumps without their bails. This comes under the category of silly but funny!

The 1908 Olympic Games were first scheduled to be held in Rome, but because of the eruption of Mount Vesuvius in 1906, they were moved to London.

Zimbabwe's women's hockey players were each rewarded with an ox when they returned home after the 1980 Olympics, having won gold.

In 1908 a Newcastle United fan named Gladstone Adams drove all the way down to Wembley to watch his team play in the FA Cup final. It was such a novelty to see a car in those days that it was put into a car showroom window while he was at the game because so many people wanted to see it. On the long way home, snow kept building up on the windscreen, which meant that Adams was continually getting out of the car to clear it. This experience led him to invent the windscreen wiper, which he patented three years later. And all because of a trip to a footie match!

Olympics onlys

Great Britain is the only country to have won at least one gold medal at every Summer Games.

The American Thomas 'Eddie' Tolan is the only man to have won a sprint gold medal while chewing gum (in 1932)!

The Finn Paavo Nurmi, winner of nine gold medals in 1920, 1924 and 1928, always ran with a stopwatch in his hand.

There are only two Olympic sports where men and women compete against each other: sailing and equestrianism.

The 1900 Olympics featured pigeon shooting. It was the first – and only – time animals were killed on purpose in an Olympic event.

In Rome, 1960, Ethiopian Abebe Bikila became the only man to win the marathon running barefoot (and was, in the process, the first black African to win a gold medal). He successfully defended his title four years later in Tokyo, but this time he wore shoes.

American Eddie Eagan, who was a boxing champion in the 1920 Games, became the only person to win gold medals in both the Summer and Winter Games when he won gold at the 1932 Winter Olympics in the team bobsled event.

Ralph Craig is the only man to have competed in two Olympic Games 36 years apart. In 1912 he ran the 100 metres. He next

competed in the 1948 Olympics at the age of 59, as an alternate in the US yachting team.

The 1912 Games were held in Stockholm, but there was no boxing as, under the (then) Swedish law, it was banned.

There are only four people who have won Olympic medals at *six* Olympic Games. Of these, the most remarkable is Germany's Birgit Fischer, a canoeist, who might have won medals at *seven* games if the country she was then representing (East Germany) hadn't boycotted the 1984 Los Angeles Games.

London is the only city to host the Olympic Games three times (1908, 1948 and 2012). Athens hosted three Games (1896, 1906 and 2004), but the 1906 Games, which were held between the regular Games of 1904 and 1908, aren't recognized by the International Olympic Committee.

In 1976 women were required to have a test to establish that they were indeed 'real' women. This was because of the huge number of body-altering drugs that Eastern European female athletes were being forced to take in order to make them tougher and stronger. Anyway, the only female competitor not to have to submit to a sex test at the 1976 Games was Princess Anne (now the Princess Royal). It was obviously felt inappropriate to ask the daughter of Queen Elizabeth II to prove that she was a princess and not, er, a prince.

Have you seen the film *Chariots of Fire*? If not, you should, as it's an extraordinary film about two athletes – Harold Abrahams and Eric Liddell – who both won gold medals at the 1924 Olympic Games. The reason I mention it here is because Harold Abrahams had been selected for the 100 metres, 200 metres and the 4 x 100m relay when, a month before the Olympics, he broke the English long jump record and was duly selected for the event. An anonymous letter then appeared in the *Daily Express* criticizing the selection of Abrahams in the long jump. Its author was Abrahams himself, who managed to withdraw from the event so that he could concentrate on his sprinting. So I suggest that Abrahams is the *only* person to be deselected from an Olympic event after sending an

anonymous letter to a newspaper demanding his deselection. Well, can you provide me with any other competitor who did such a thing?

In 1908 Wyndham Halswelle, a British veteran of the Boer War, became the only Olympian to win a gold medal (in the 400 metres) without any opponents. In the first, void race, Halswelle was obstructed by John Carpenter, an American who crossed the line first but was disqualified. Carpenter's American team-mates refused to take part in the re-run and so Halswelle ran a solo race.

There have been two deaths at the Summer Olympics.

Knud Enemark Jensen (Rome, 1960): the Danish cyclist collapsed during the 100km team time trial, fatally fracturing his skull. The autopsy showed he had taken performance-enhancing drugs which might have caused his fall – though the weather, a blistering 33 degrees Celsius, would definitely have been a contributory factor. In fact, the official cause of death was given as heat stroke. His death led the IOC to form a medical commission to begin drug testing.

Francisco Lazaro (Stockholm, 1912): the Portuguese marathon runner collapsed from sunstroke and heart trouble, and died the next day.

In 1952 Emil Zátopek of Czechoslovakia became the only man to win gold medals in the 5,000 metres, the 10,000 metres and the marathon in the same Olympic Games – setting Olympic records in *all* these events. Incredibly, and you might find this hard to believe, Zátopek *had never run a marathon before*.

1900 was the first – and only – time that the Olympic swimming events were held in a river. It's true: the Paris swimming events were held in the River Seine, which meant that the contestants had to contend with the current. In the Seine? In *sane*, more like!

BBC Sports Personality of the Year

This is probably the most important award a British sports person can win as it is voted for by the viewers – i.e. the fans. It was started in 1954. In 2009 the footballer Ryan Giggs received the most votes to win the award. This was unusual as he was a member of a team (Manchester United), and most years the award goes to an individual sportsman or -woman. To give you an idea of how true that is, let's look at a breakdown of the sports from which the winners have come.

Athletics:	17
Motor Racing:	6
Boxing:	5
Cricket:	5
Football:	5
Ice Skating:	3
Tennis:	3
Cycling:	2
Eventing:	2
Golf:	2
Swimming:	2

Motorcycle Racing:	1
Rowing:	1
Rugby Union:	1
Show Jumping:	1
Snooker:	1
Horse racing:	1

Out of 58 awards, only 11 recipients have been team players (though you can add two more if you consider rower Sir Steve Redgrave to be a team member rather than an individual, and if you think that skaters Torvill and Dean, the winners in 1984, are a team rather than a pair of individuals). This bias towards individual sports means that football and cricket, our two national sports, are rather under-represented.

Here are all the winners from 1954 to 2009. It should go without saying that all of them deserved their awards, but it's equally true to say that very often the award has gone to someone whose sporting achievement happened to be on television.

1954 Chris Chataway (athletics)
1955 Gordon Pirie (athletics)
1956 Jim Laker (cricket)

1957 Dai Rees (golf)
1958 Ian Black (swimming)
1959 John Surtees (motor racing)
1960 David Broome (show jumping)
1961 Stirling Moss (motor racing)
1962 Anita Lonsbrough (swimming)
1963 Dorothy Hyman (athletics)
1964 Mary Rand (athletics)
1965 Tommy Simpson (cycling)
1966 Bobby Moore (football)
1967 Henry Cooper (boxing)
1968 David Hemery (athletics)
1969 Ann Jones (tennis)
1970 Henry Cooper (boxing)
1971 Princess Anne (eventing)
1972 Mary Peters (athletics)
1973 Jackie Stewart (motor racing)
1974 Brendan Foster (athletics)
1975 David Steele (cricket)
1976 John Curry (ice skating)
1977 Virginia Wade (tennis)
1978 Steve Ovett (athletics)
1979 Sebastian Coe (athletics)
1980 Robin Cousins (ice skating)
1981 Ian Botham (cricket)
1982 Daley Thompson (athletics)
1983 Steve Cram (athletics)

1984 **Torvill and Dean (ice skating)**
1985 Barry McGuigan (boxing)
1986 **Nigel Mansell (motor racing)**
1987 Fatima Whitbread (athletics)
1988 **Steve Davis (snooker)**
1989 Nick Faldo (golf)
1990 Paul Gascoigne (football)
1991 Liz McColgan (athletics)
1992 **Nigel Mansell (motor racing)**
1993 Linford Christie (athletics)
1994 **Damon Hill (motor racing)**
1995 Jonathan Edwards (athletics)
1996 **Damon Hill (motor racing)**
1997 Greg Rusedski (tennis)
1998 **Michael Owen (football)**
1999 Lennox Lewis (boxing)
2000 **Steve Redgrave (rowing)**
2001 David Beckham (football)
2002 **Paula Radcliffe (athletics)**
2003 Jonny Wilkinson (rugby)
2004 **Kelly Holmes (athletics)**
2005 Andrew Flintoff (cricket)
2006 **Zara Phillips (eventing)**
2007 Joe Calzaghe (boxing)
2008 **Chris Hoy (cycling)**
2009 Ryan Giggs (football)
2010 **Tony McCoy (jockey)**

HERE ARE SOME OF THE GREAT PEOPLE WHO *DIDN'T* WIN IT

Sir Roger Bannister (athletics) (was voted second once)

Geoffrey Boycott (cricket) (second once)

George Best (football) (second once and third once)

Lewis Hamilton (motor racing) (second twice)

Jenson Button (motor racing) (second once)

Gary Lineker (football) (third once)

Lester Piggott (horse racing)

Martin Johnson (rugby union)

Sir Geoff Hurst (football) (third once)

Graham Hill (motor racing) (second once)

Sir Bobby Charlton (football) (second twice)

David Gower (cricket)

However, there *are* other awards presented alongside the Sports Personality of the Year Award, and these occasionally include

the Special Achievement Award. This was first awarded in 1981 to Dennis Moore for completing the very first London Marathon despite being blind since birth.

The only other winners of this award are jockey Lester Piggott – twice (in 1984 and 1994), comedian David Walliams in 2006 'for his outstanding achievement of swimming the English Channel for charity' (raising over £1 million for Sport Relief), and comedian Eddie Izzard in 2009 after running 43 marathons in 51 days for Sport Relief.

Oldest

It is every golfer's ambition to 'score his age' – that's to say, go around a golf course in the same number of strokes (or fewer) as his age. The oldest player to 'score his age' in a game of golf was C. Arthur Thompson (1869–1975) of Victoria, British Columbia, Canada, who carded 103 in 1973. I think most of us would agree that managing to play golf at all over the age of 100 is an immense achievement – irrespective of the score!

The world's oldest Test cricketer was England's Wilfred Rhodes, who was 52 years and 165 days old at the end of his final Test against the West Indies in 1930. Having begun his Test career at the age of just 21, Rhodes could also boast the world's longest Test career: 30 years and 315 days.

Sheffield Football Club, founded in 1857, is the world's oldest football club still in existence. When it started, the team played its own code of football: the Sheffield rules, in which players were allowed to hit the ball with their hands. The code dwindled

out in the 1870s but the club still carried on. Currently, Sheffield FC play in the Northern Premier League Division One South.

Queen's Park is the oldest Scottish club, having been founded in 1867. Its home is Hampden Park, which is also where Scotland play their home games. Queen's Park, who play in the Scottish Third Division, are now the only amateur club in the whole of the Scottish League. In fact, their amateur status is enshrined in their motto, *Ludere Causa Ludendi*, which translates from Latin to mean 'to play for the sake of playing'.

Sir Stanley Matthews is the oldest ever soccer international. He was over 42 when he played for England against Denmark in 1957. He was 50 when he played his final game for Stoke City in 1965, making him, by far, not only the oldest man to play in top flight football (Stoke were then in the First Division – the equivalent of today's Premier League) but also the oldest to appear in a professional football match in Britain. It's even more extraordinary when you think that he wasn't a goalkeeper or a defender (who might perhaps need less stamina) but a winger!

Leslie Compton became the oldest player to make his debut for the England football team when he played against Wales in 1950 at the age of 38 years and two months.

The Swedish marksman Oscar Swahn is the oldest man to have competed at the Olympics. He won the last of his six Olympic medals (a silver in the running deer, double shot team event) in the 1920 Antwerp Games at the age of 72 years and 280 days. Obviously, this also makes him the oldest Olympic medallist.

The British equestrian Lorna Johnstone is the oldest woman to have competed at the Olympics. She was 70 years and five days old when she rode at the 1972 Games.

The oldest football in existence is the one displayed in the Stirling Smith Museum in Scotland. It is over 450 years old and made from an outer casing of deerskin containing a pig's bladder. It is claimed that it was once the property of Mary, Queen of Scots.

The oldest sporting trophy that is still being competed for is the America's Cup, which is for yacht racing. It started in 1851, and certainly lived up to its name, with the Americans winning for a straight 132 years until Australia took the Cup in 1983.

The oldest jockey to win the Grand National was Dick Saunders, aged 48, on Grittar in 1982.

Youngest

Greek gymnast Dimitrios Loundras is the youngest person ever to have taken part in the Olympics. He was just 10 years old when he represented his country in the gymnastics at the first modern Olympics in 1896.

I say that Dimitrios Loundras is the youngest competitor, but there's speculation that the young French boy who was brought in to cox (i.e. steer) the Dutch pair in the 1900 rowing final might have been even younger. What happened was that the Dutch rowers thought that their cox was, at 60kg, too heavy, and so they drafted in a local lad (the Games were held in Paris that year). So far, so true – and, indeed, there is a photograph in existence of the two oarsmen with the boy after they'd won the gold medal (so it was evidently a good idea). However, despite exhaustive research, no one has ever identified the boy or his age – though it's thought he might have been as young as seven!

In 1982, at the age of 17 years and 47 days, Norman Whiteside (of Manchester United and Northern Ireland) became the youngest player ever to play in the World Cup finals.

14-year-old Abdi Abdifatah of Somalia was the youngest of the 5,602 players who featured in the 2010 football World Cup qualifying matches (the oldest was 43-year-old Kenny Dyer of Montserrat).

Germany's Sebastian Vettel is the youngest man ever to win the Formula One World Driver's Championship. He won the title in 2010 at the age of 23 years and 135 days, beating the record set by Britain's Lewis Hamilton in 2008 by 166 days.

The youngest jockey to win the Grand National was Bruce Hobbs, aged 17, on Battleship in 1938.

When 17-year-old Andy Murray was called up to play doubles for Great Britain's Davis Cup team in March 2005, he became Britain's youngest ever Davis Cup player.

Some Olympic medallists who became film stars

Carl Lewis (gold in the 100 metres, 1984 and 1988) had acting roles in films like *Tournament of Dreams* and *Material Girls*.

Johnny Weissmuller (swimming gold, 1924 and 1928) starred in *Tarzan, the Ape Man* and went on to become the most famous Tarzan actor of them all.

Muhammad Ali (boxing gold, 1960) played himself in *The Greatest* and also acted in the film *Freedom Road*.

Onlys (1)

Frank Hayes is the only jockey to win a race after death. No, really! It was 1923, and poor Frank suffered a fatal heart attack in the middle of a race at Belmont Park in New York. However, his horse, Sweet Kiss, didn't know this and carried on to win the race with the lifeless jockey still on board.

Danny Clapton is the only footballer to play for England *and* his club on the same day. On 26 November 1958 Clapton played for England against Wales at Villa Park in the afternoon, and then, in the evening, for Arsenal in a friendly against Juventus. Jack Kelsey is the only footballer to play for Wales *and* his club on the same day. And guess what? It was the same day! Clapton and Kelsey (the Wales goalkeeper) were both driven from Villa Park to Highbury (Arsenal's ground at that time) to play in the evening.

Alan Mullally is the only England Test cricketer to have four of the same letter in his surname.

Antonio Carbajal, the Mexican goalkeeper, is the only man to play in five World Cups (in the final stages) – from 1950–1966. It earned him the nickname 'El Cinco Copas' (the Five Cups).

Only two players – Pele (Brazil) and Uwe Seeler (West Germany) – have *scored* in four consecutive football World Cup finals – and, interestingly, both players scored during the same four World Cups (1958–1970).

Jack MacBryan is the only Test cricketer never to have batted, bowled or taken a catch in his entire Test career. He played his only Test for England in 1924, but very few (just 66.5) overs were possible because of the rain, and poor Jack never got a look in!

Only two football World Cups have been held outside the Americas and Europe: 2002 (South Korea/Japan), and 2010 (South Africa).

Only two greys (which is how white horses are known) have won the Grand National: The Lamb in 1868 and 1871, and Nicolaus Silver in 1961.

There are only two families who have played Test cricket in three consecutive generations. George Headley, one of the greatest batsmen of all time, and his son Ron both played Test cricket for the West Indies, and Ron's son Dean played for England. Jahangir Khan played Test cricket for India while his son, Majid, and grandson, Bazid, both played for Pakistan.

Neil Paterson is the only British footballer to win an Oscar. He played for Dundee United in the 1940s while also working as a freelance writer. In 1959 he won the Oscar for his screenplay for *Room at the Top*.

Manchester City are the only League club to have scored and conceded a century of goals in a single season. In 1957–58 they scored 104 goals but conceded 100.

Alan Shearer is the only player since the Second World War to have scored more than 30 top-division goals in three successive seasons – 31 in 1993–94, 34 in 1994–95 and 31 in 1995–96.

The American tennis player Bobby Riggs only played Wimbledon once – in 1939 – but left with the perfect record, winning the singles, the doubles and the mixed doubles. Always a hustler, he played deliberately badly in a pre-Wimbledon tournament and then backed himself with bookmakers at high odds to win Wimbledon. Nowadays he's probably best remembered for challenging the then women's champion Billie-Jean King in a famous 'Battle of the Sexes'. He lost – but, to be fair, he was 55 at the time and it remains the most-watched tennis match in television history.

Regular readers will know that Hull City is the only British football team that hasn't got any letters you can fill in with a pen. Along similar lines, Dundee is the only British professional club with a name that doesn't contain any letters that appear in the word 'football'.

R. E. 'Tip' Foster is the only man to captain England at both football and cricket. He also still holds the world record for the highest score on Test debut – having scored 287 for England against Australia in 1903–04.

Heroes

By any definition, the Welsh international rugby union player Harry Jarman was a huge hero. In 1928 he spotted a runaway coal truck heading towards a group of children playing. Without a thought for his own safety, he threw himself in front of the children and saved them. Alas, he died doing so, but what a truly great man.

The great Liberian international footballer George Weah paid for all his team's uniforms and other expenses so that Liberia could compete in the 1996 Africa Cup of Nations.

Having been a pilot in the First World War, the Frenchman Robert Benoist became a Grand Prix motor-racing driver. He enjoyed huge success in his career, but that's not the reason for his inclusion in this section. No, that's because of his activities in the Second World War. On the outbreak of war, he and two other racing drivers escaped to England, where they joined the SOE (Special Operations Executive) and became secret agents in order to return to France to assist

the French Resistance. Parachuted into France, Captain Benoist helped organize sabotage cells and moved weapons from air-drops in the forest to his home for storage and distribution. Unfortunately the Gestapo (the German secret police) caught him, but while being driven to Gestapo headquarters, Benoist leaped from the moving vehicle and escaped, eventually being smuggled back to Britain via the French underground.

You'd think that would have been enough excitement for one man, but Benoist insisted on returning to France for a second mission, and then a third. On this occasion he was captured and, on 11 September 1944, executed.

After the war the Coupe Robert Benoist automobile race was held in Paris in his memory and a street was named after him.

At the 1904 Olympics the American gymnast George Eyser won six medals – even though his left leg was made out of wood.

Sometimes a loser can become a winner if enough people take him to their hearts. This was the case with Eddie 'the Eagle' Edwards, whose valiant – but doomed – attempts in the ski-jump in the 1988 Winter Olympics endeared him to people all over the world.

Similarly, at the 2000 Summer Olympics, a swimmer from Equatorial Guinea, Eric Moussambani – nicknamed 'the Eel' – became a hero. He took 112.72 seconds in the 100m freestyle, which was more than twice as long as the winner, but he had only recently learned to swim and had never trained in a full-length pool so the public took him to their hearts.

There are many heroes and heroines who compete at the Paralympics. All of them have extraordinary stories to tell about how they've overcome their disabilities to become fine sportsmen and -women. However, South African swimmer Natalie du Toit, whose left leg was amputated following a motor-scooter accident, stands out as a special heroine. Having won five gold medals at the Athens Paralympics in 2004, she qualified to compete at the 2008 Beijing Olympics – making history by becoming the first amputee to qualify for the Olympic Games since Olivér Halassy in 1936. She was able to compete in the Olympics rather than the Paralympics because she doesn't use a prosthetic leg when she's swimming and so can't be accused of having an advantage – as, for example, an athlete with an artificial leg might when running. She came 16th (out of 25 competitors) in the 10km 'marathon' swim. Incidentally, South Africa's Olympic Committee chose Natalie to carry their flag at the 2008 Summer Olympics opening ceremony, making her the first athlete to carry a flag in both the Olympics and the Paralympics in the same year.

Similarly, the Polish athlete Natalia Partyka, who was born without a right forearm, competed in table tennis in both the 2008 Olympic Games and the 2008 Paralympic Games.

Jeff Hall, who played football for Birmingham City and England, died of polio just two weeks after being taken ill in March 1958. The publicity surrounding his death helped to persuade people to participate in a mass inoculation scheme to combat the awful disease. So a man who was a sporting hero in life (England never lost a game in which he played) became an even greater hero in death.

Villains

James Snook won two gold medals for shooting at the 1920 Olympics and went on to become a professor of veterinary medicine at Ohio State University. So far, so good, but in 1928 Snook murdered his girlfriend, and eight months later was executed in the electric chair.

In 1972 an entire football team in Córdoba, Argentina, was jailed after the players kicked a linesman to death.

Leslie Hylton was a fast bowler who played in six Test matches for the West Indies between 1935 and 1939. In 1955 he was hanged for murdering his wife. He is the only Test cricketer to have been executed.

In the 1988 Olympics, the Canadian runner Ben Johnson won the 100m sprint in a world-record time of 9.79 seconds. Shortly afterwards he tested positive for steroid use and was stripped of his medal.

In 1930 Alex Villaplane captained France to

victory in the very first match of the very first football World Cup. 14 years later, he was shot by a French firing squad for collaborating with the Nazis.

There was a scandal at the 1980 Boston Marathon when an amateur runner named Rosie Ruiz appeared from out of nowhere to win the women's race. Marathon officials became suspicious when it was found that Ruiz didn't appear in race videotapes until near the end of the race. A subsequent investigation decided that Ruiz had skipped most of the race and blended into the crowd about one mile from the finish line, where she then ran to her apparent victory. Ruiz was officially disqualified. And quite rightly too!

Some football clubs and their mascots – past and present

Arsenal: Gunnersaurus Rex
Birmingham City: Beau Brummie
Blackburn Rovers: Roar Lion
Bolton: Lofty Lion
Chelsea: Stamford Lion
Fulham: Billy the Badger
Leeds United: Lucas the Kop Kat
Leicester City: Filbert Fox
Manchester City: Moonchester
Manchester United: Fred the Red
Middlesbrough: Roary the Lion
Newcastle United: Monty Magpie
Norwich City: Captain Canary
Nottingham Forest: Sherwood Bear
Sheffield Wednesday: Ozzie the Owl
Southampton: Super Saint
Tottenham Hotspur: Chirpy Cockerel
West Bromwich Albion: Baggie Bird
West Ham United: Bubbles the Bear
Wolverhampton Wanderers: Wolfie

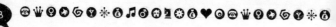

Bad sportsmanship

'If you win through bad sportsmanship, that's no real victory' – Babe Didrikson Zaharias, American athlete.

The Ryder Cup is an important bi-annual golf match between the US and Europe. In 1999 it went right down to the wire. At the very last hole, the American golfer Justin Leonard sank a long putt and the American team and their supporters went wild – dancing all over the green . . . which would have been fine but for the fact that European golfer José María Olazábal still had a (difficult) shot to tie the match. Inevitably all the whooping put him off and the Americans won the match and the Cup – but not without upsetting their opponents; the European golfer later describing the US celebrations as 'a very ugly picture to see'.

American golfers were guilty of a similar act of bad sportsmanship the very next year. Or should that be sports*womanship*, as the Solheim Cup is the women's equivalent to the Ryder Cup. In 2000 a European golfer

named Annika Sorenstam had a very difficult shot for a birdie (as a one-under-par score is known). As she got herself ready, she was watched by both teams. Finally she took the shot, and sank the birdie. However, at that point the US team – which, remember, had been watching the action – complained to the referee that it had been the Americans' turn to putt (as they had been further from the hole), and that the birdie shouldn't count. The referee agreed, and the European golfer was forced to retake the shot. Understandably, she missed the putt, and the Europeans went on to lose the Solheim Cup by one shot.

You might recall that England played Germany in the last 16 of the 2010 FIFA World Cup. In the event, we lost fair and square. However, the game was marred by the fact that Frank Lampard had a perfectly good goal disallowed in the first half. The referee – and his assistants – simply didn't see that the ball had crossed the line by at least a metre before ricocheting out again. One person who knew for sure – that's one person *apart* from all the millions watching on TV – that the ball had crossed the line was the German goalkeeper, Manuel Neuer. However, instead of owning up, he did his very best to deliberately fool the officials into thinking that he'd saved the ball on the line without allowing it across.

If England – who were 2–1 down at the time – had equalized at that point, who knows what might have happened next: maybe the momentum would have led to another goal – and then another. Instead, they lost the match 4–1.

So was German goalkeeper Manuel Neuer guilty of bad sportsmanship?

I'm not sure.

It would have taken a huge amount of courage – and self-sacrifice – in what is, after all, a team game, to have told the referee that the ball had crossed the line.

Having said that, he did try to make it look like he had saved the ball and had the situation under control.

I think, on balance, that we can't expect more from professional footballers – especially those playing in a high-stakes game (and they don't come much higher than the World Cup) – than that they don't *actively* cheat, and allow the referee to control the game: in other words, play to the whistle.

What we *can* say for sure is that, even

if Manuel Neuer wasn't guilty of bad sportsmanship, to have owned up would have been an act of supremely *good* sportsmanship.

In 1981 Australia were playing New Zealand in a one-day cricket international. There was just one ball left to be bowled in the match and New Zealand needed six runs to tie the match. The Australian captain, Greg Chappell, ordered the bowler, Trevor Chappell (his brother) to bowl underarm – which made it virtually impossible for the batsman to hit because it was so low. The batsmen walked off in disgust and the then New Zealand Prime Minister called it 'the most disgusting incident I can recall in the history of cricket', going on to say, 'It was an act of cowardice and I consider it appropriate that the Australian team were wearing yellow.'

As a direct result of the Chappell brothers' action, underarm bowling was ruled illegal.

In a group match in the 2002 football World Cup between Turkey and Brazil, the Brazilians, who were in the lead, were awarded a free kick. Rivaldo went about his business very slowly in order to waste time. Understandably, a Turkish player, frustrated by the delay, kicked the ball towards Rivaldo, to speed things up. The ball hit Rivaldo on the shins, but he clutched his face, and collapsed to the ground. The referee, who hadn't seen the incident, mistakenly thought that Rivaldo had been hit in the face and sent the Turkish player off. The 10-man Turkish team subsequently lost the game.

In the last race of the 1994 Formula One season, Michael Schumacher was leading the table by a single point from Damon Hill. This meant that Hill would win the World Championship if he finished anywhere in front of Schumacher. Towards the end of the race Schumacher was in the lead, closely followed by Hill. Schumacher made a mistake in one of his turns, which left room for Hill to pass him on the inside. Hill started to overtake Schumacher, and got about halfway past when Schumacher slammed his car into Hill's, crashing both cars. This meant that neither could complete the race. That being the case, Schumacher finished the season a point ahead of Hill, and therefore won the World Championship.

In 1986 – just four years after the Falklands conflict between the two countries – England and Argentina were drawn to play against each other at the football World Cup. Alas, it was soured by an act of supremely bad sportsmanship. The Argentinian striker Diego Maradona, widely acclaimed as the best player in the world, knocked the ball into the goal with his hand. The referee didn't see

this, awarded the goal, and Argentina went on to win the match (admittedly after a later sublime goal by Maradona). The TV cameras, however, had captured Maradona's act, and he was asked about it after the game. His reply? 'It was partly the head of Maradona, and partly the Hand of God.' Later, Maradona admitted to what the rest of the world knew: that it was a hand ball or, in other words, a blatant piece of cheating.

Muhammad Ali is not just the greatest boxer of all time but also widely recognized as the greatest ever sporting hero. However, when he fought Britain's much-loved Henry Cooper in 1963, he and his 'corner' (as a boxer's back-up team is known) resorted to a bit of bad sportsmanship. In the fourth round Cooper knocked Ali to the floor with his famous punch nicknamed 'Henry's hammer'. Before Cooper could go for the knockout, the bell rang for the end of the round. The stunned Ali needed more than a minute (the interval between rounds) to recover, and so his trainer ripped his glove in order to gain time while the glove (which, to be fair, had had a tiny rip before the fight) was repaired. It only took a few seconds, but it enabled Ali to get his act together and go on to win the contest. You might be interested to know that, as a result of this incident, each corner is now required to have a spare pair of gloves.

In a game of football, when there's an injury, players tend to kick the ball off the field so that the injured player can be attended to. Then, when play resumes, the convention is that the ball is returned to the team

which had been in possession. However, a man named Fernando de Moraes rather undermined that idea when, playing for South Melbourne FC in a 2009 match against Sunshine Georgies FC, he indulged in a piece of poor sportsmanship. Having thrown the ball to the opposition's goalie (as was usual), Moraes crept up behind him, stole the ball and scored. Tut tut!

This was similar to what had happened 10 years earlier in a fifth-round FA Cup match between Arsenal and Sheffield United in 1999. After the Sheffield United keeper, Alan Kelly, had kicked the ball out so that an injured player could get treatment, Arsenal's Ray Parlour threw the ball back to the keeper. However, Arsenal's Nwankwo Kanu, not realizing what was going on, intercepted the ball and crossed it to Marc Overmars, who scored to give Arsenal a 2–1 lead just 10 minutes from time. And that's how the game ended.

To his immense credit, Arsenal's manager, Arsène Wenger, offered to replay the match, which ended in another 2–1 victory to Arsenal – but at least honour was satisfied.

For really bad sportsmanship, you have to look no further than the sport of boxing. When Mike Tyson fought Evander Holyfield in 1997, he took a bite out of Holyfield's ear and spat it onto the floor. This was noticed by the referee and Tyson was penalized. However, just seconds later he tried to bite Holyfield's ear a second time and was disqualified while Holyfield was named the winner.

If bad sportsmanship extends to stealing or receiving secret information about your opponents, then the Formula One team McLaren stands guilty of that. In 2007 they were accused of obtaining secret technical information from the Ferrari team the year before. They were fined $100 million and excluded from the 2007 Constructors' Championship.

Perhaps the worst (or *best*, if you stop to think about it!) example of bad sportsmanship was exhibited by Cuba's Ángel Valodia Matos at the 2008 Olympics. After being disqualified from his bronze medal bout with Kazakhstan's Arman Chilmanov in the tae kwon do, he lashed out at a referee and a judge. He even kicked the Swedish judge in the head! Now *that's* what you call a poor loser . . .

Understandably, he was banned from the Olympics for life.

Good sportsmanship

'One man practising good sportsmanship is far better than 50 others preaching it' – Knute Rockne, American football player.

'Sportsmanship for me is when a guy walks off the court and you really can't tell whether he won or lost, when he carries himself with pride either way' – Jim Courier, American tennis player.

Let me start with my favourite story about great sportsmanship. Back in 1969, the Ryder Cup was contested between the US and Great Britain and Ireland (nowadays the US's opponents are Europe, which makes for a much closer encounter). The Americans had won the previous five times. In the final singles match on the final day, with the two teams all square, Jack Nicklaus (US) and Tony Jacklin (GB) were on the final green. Nicklaus sank his final putt, leaving Jacklin with a short putt to tie the match and the whole contest. To everyone's amazement – including that of his captain, Sam Snead – Nicklaus conceded the putt, saying, 'Tony, I don't think for a second you're going to miss that putt. But I'm not going to give you the chance.' It was an extraordinary gesture: if Jacklin had missed it, the US would have won the Cup.

Eight years later, Jack Nicklaus once again showed that being an incredibly tough competitor didn't rule out good sportsmanship. It was the (British) Open Championship of 1977, and Nicklaus and Tom Watson went head to head in the greatest display of golf I've ever seen. When Tom Watson holed the winning putt, he was congratulated by his opponent. As Watson later said, 'As we walked off, Jack grabbed me by the neck and darn near broke it. He said, "Tom, I gave it my best shot, but it wasn't good enough. Congratulations. I'm proud of you." That's Jack in defeat. He always gives credit and he does it with a genuine grace. I've always respected Jack for that more than anything else. Jack was the most gracious competitor I've ever seen in the throes of defeat. I've never seen somebody be able to take defeat and, even though he's hurting inside, give credit to the player who beat him.'

The American swimmer Aaron Peirsol won the 200m backstroke at the 2004 Olympics but was disqualified because of a technical fault – an illegal turn. The Austrian Markus Rogan, who had finished second, was declared the winner but told the world's press that he didn't want the gold medal: 'It does not belong to me. Peirsol is the best, he deserves it.' A few minutes later, following an appeal, the disqualified Peirsol was reinstated as the winner, but nothing can take away the sportsmanship – and dignity – of Markus Rogan.

And he got his reward: at the end of the year he was voted Austria's Sportsman of the Year.

At the 1964 Winter Olympics the British two-man bob team of Tony Nash and Robin Dixon won the gold medal – but only after one of the greatest moments of sportsmanship ever seen. In second place after their first run, Nash and Dixon realized they had broken a bolt in their rear axle, effectively putting them out of the competition. Step forward the great Italian bobsled driver Eugenio Monti, who was in first place. Without hesitation, he removed the bolt from the rear axle of his own sled and sent it up to Nash and Dixon, who repaired their sled and went on to win gold. Monti and his partner took the bronze.

Afterwards, Monti said of his fellow driver, 'Tony Nash did not win because I gave him a bolt. Tony Nash won because he was the best driver.'

Incredibly, at the same Olympics, Monti also helped the Canadian four-man team to repair their sled, and they too won gold, with Monti and his team again having to be satisfied with bronze.

For his actions, Monti became the first winner of the Pierre de Coubertin International Fair Play Trophy.

You might be interested to know that Eugenio Monti eventually won two golds at the 1968 Winter Olympics at the age of 40!

One of the most sporting cricketers I've ever seen was India's Gundappa Viswanath. In the 1980 Jubilee Test, England were struggling on 85 for 5 when Bob Taylor was given out caught behind. Incredibly, Viswanath, the Indian captain, pleaded with the umpires to recall Taylor because he thought the batsman was not out. Taylor returned to forge a match-winning partnership with Ian Botham.

In 2001 the Italian Paolo Di Canio was playing for West Ham United at Everton. At the end, deep into injury time, the game was deadlocked when Paul Gerrard, the Everton goalkeeper, ran out of his area to collect the ball. In doing so, he twisted his knee and fell to the ground. Di Canio's team-mate, Trevor Sinclair, got to the ball and passed it to Di Canio to put it in the net for a goal and a win. Instead, Di Canio caught the ball, pointing at the stricken keeper. Sepp Blatter, the FIFA president, congratulated Di Canio 'for this splendid gesture made in the true spirit of fair play', and at the end of the season Di Canio was given the FIFA Fair Play Award.

In 2008, at the Beijing Olympics, Dara Torres became the first American swimmer to compete in five Olympic Games, but it was her actions while there that concern us here. She was taking part in a preliminary heat for the 50m freestyle. As she and her rivals took their positions for the start, the swimsuit of one of her rivals tore. Dara tried to help, but the rip couldn't be repaired on the spot and the woman needed to change her swimsuit. Obviously this would take so much time that the woman would miss the race – and her chance to compete in the Olympics, something for which she would have trained for many years. So Dara Torres, instead of staying focused on her imminent race, got

down from the block and went to tell the officials that the race would have to be delayed. The competitor eventually returned and the race took place without any absences – all thanks to the fair-mindedness of Dara Torres.

Mention the name Tana Umaga, legend of the All Blacks (as the New Zealand rugby union team are known), and many people will recall his infamous spear tackle on Brian O'Driscoll, which put the British Lions captain out for the whole of the 2005 series. But Umaga is also entitled to be remembered for his sportsmanship. In a 2003 Test match against Wales, the Welsh captain, Colin Charvis, was knocked out after a typically tough All Blacks tackle. This put the New Zealanders on the attack, with a strong chance of scoring a try, but Umaga stopped playing to check that Charvis had not swallowed his mouthguard. That deserves to be remembered as much as the spear tackle.

Here's a heartwarming tale that comes from a 2003 international soccer match between Denmark and Iran. Approaching half-time, an Iranian player thought he heard the referee's whistle and so picked up the ball to give it to him. However, it wasn't the ref but someone in the crowd. Because the player had handled the ball in his own penalty area, the referee had no option but to award Denmark a penalty. To their credit, the Danes didn't like this one bit, and so, after a quick conversation with their coach, a player went up to take the penalty and deliberately kicked it wide.

Acts of sportsmanship are all very well when a team – or a player – is going to win anyway, but they're extra special when they come at a cost. When the American tennis player Andy Roddick was playing Fernando Verdasco of Spain in the 2005 Rome Masters, his sportsmanship cost him a shot at the tournament. Roddick was one set up, and leading 5–3 in the second set (they were playing the best of three), with three match points, when Verdasco double-faulted to lose the point and the match. However, Roddick overruled the line judge and the umpire, and declared that the second serve was good and therefore the point should be awarded to his opponent. From that position, Verdasco went on to win the match – thereby eliminating Roddick from the tournament.

The American Al Oerter was a discus legend. As the defending Olympic champion at the 1960 Rome Olympics, he was the slight favourite over his team-mate Rink Babka, even though Babka was the world record holder.

After four rounds, Babka was in the lead. What happened next is a wonderful example of sportsmanship. As Oerter prepared to take his fifth throw, Babka gave him advice that enabled him to throw his discus so far that he won the gold medal, setting a new Olympic record. Babka took silver, and never regretted giving Oerter the benefit of his wisdom.

Oerter went on to win gold again in 1964 and 1968.

Here's a lovely story with which to finish this section. The Australian Henry Pearce was competing in the single scull rowing event at the 1928 Olympics, and was in the lead when a duck and her ducklings came into view on a collision course. Pearce had a choice: carry on rowing and kill a couple of ducklings, or pull in his oars and let them pass. He chose the latter, and yet still went on to win the race. It goes to show that nice guys don't always finish last!

The recipients of FIFA World Player of the Year Award

2010: Lionel Messi
2009: Lionel Messi
2008: Cristiano Ronaldo
2007: Kaká
2006: Fabio Cannavaro
2005: Ronaldinho
2004: Ronaldinho
2003: Zinédine Zidane
2002: Ronaldo
2001: Luís Figo
2000: Zinédine Zidane
1999: Rivaldo
1998: Zinédine Zidane
1997: Ronaldo
1996: Ronaldo
1995: George Weah
1994: Romário
1993: Roberto Baggio
1992: Marco Van Basten
1991: Lothar Matthäus

No British player has yet been voted FIFA World Player of the Year, but David Beckham twice finished second, Frank Lampard once finished second, and Alan Shearer and Gary Lineker each once came third.

World Soccer Magazine's Young Players of the Year

2010: Thomas Müller, Bayern Munich
(with 46 per cent of the votes cast)

2009: Sergio Agüero, Atlético Madrid
(45 per cent)

2008: Lionel Messi, Barcelona (44 per cent)

2007: Lionel Messi, Barcelona (34 per cent)

2006: Lionel Messi, Barcelona (36 per cent)

2005: Robinho, Santos (30 per cent)

The great baseball player Yogi Berra became well-known for his wonderful witticisms, which didn't always come out as he intended. Here are a selection of them:

'Always go to other people's funerals; otherwise they won't go to yours.'

'I knew the record would stand until it was broken.'

'If the world were perfect, it wouldn't be.'

'If you don't know where you're going, you might not get there.'

'It gets late awfully early around here.'

'It's *déjà vu* all over again.'

'Ninety per cent of this game is mental, and the other half is physical.'

'A nickel ain't worth a dime any more.'

'Half the lies they tell about me aren't true.'

'I'd give my right arm to be ambidextrous.'

'I knew I was going to take the wrong train, so I left early.'

'I usually take a two-hour nap from one to four.'

'If I didn't wake up, I'd still be sleeping.'

'It ain't over till it's over.'

'Never answer an anonymous letter.'

'Steve McQueen looks good in this movie. He must have made it before he died.'

'Surprise me!' (when his wife asked whether he would like to be buried or cremated)

'The other team could make trouble for us if they win.'

'Why buy good luggage? You only use it when you travel.'

'You have to give 100 per cent in the first half of the game. If that isn't enough, in the second half you have to give what's left.'

'I can't concentrate when I'm thinking.'

Yogi Berra's British equivalent is Murray Walker. Now retired from Formula One Grand Prix commentating, Murray was prone to the odd hilarious mistake. Here are some of his greatest gaffes:

'I don't make mistakes. I make prophecies which immediately turn out to be wrong' (Murray on his style of commentary).

'The lead car is absolutely unique – except for the one behind it, which is identical.'

'Now excuse me while I interrupt myself.'

'Schumacher – he is either coming into the pits on this lap or he is not.'

'So, with half the race gone there's half the race to go.'

'I make no apologies for their absence – I'm sorry they're not here.'

'This is lap 54. After that, it's 55, 56, 57, 58 . . .'

'I imagine that the conditions in those cars

today are totally unimaginable.'

'The atmosphere is so tense you could cut it with a cricket stump.'

'The status quo could well be as it was before.'

'Either the car is stationary or it's on the move.'

'Patrick Tambay's hopes, which were nil before, are absolutely zero now.'

'He's obviously gone in for a wheel change. I say obviously because I can't see it.'

'Anything happens in Grand Prix racing and it usually does.'

'He is shedding buckets of adrenalin in that car.'

'It's raining and the track is wet.'

'. . . and there's no damage to the car . . . except to the car itself.'

'Unless I'm very much mistaken . . . I *am* very much mistaken!'

'Only a few more laps to go and then the

action will begin, unless this is the action, which it is.'

'And the first five places are filled by five different cars.'

'The lead is now 6.9 seconds. In fact it's just under seven seconds.'

'Andrea de Cesaris . . . the man who has won more Grands Prix than anyone else without actually winning one of them.'

Sporting origins

The Football League was established for the 1888–89 season with just 12 teams: Preston North End, Aston Villa, Wolverhampton Wanderers, Blackburn Rovers, Bolton Wanderers, West Bromwich Albion, Accrington (no relation to Accrington Stanley), Everton, Burnley, Derby County, Notts County and Stoke City. Preston North End won the first title without suffering a single defeat.

The game of cricket has been traced back to shepherds in 17th-century England. The shepherds would bat in front of a tree stump – hence the term 'stumps'. Sometimes a game was played in front of a wicket-gate – hence the term 'wickets'.

The first laws of cricket were written in 1774, since when there have been many changes. The early cricket bat was a long curved piece of wood like a thick hockey stick. The stumps consisted of two wickets with a single bail in between. The only law of the game that has remained constant is the length of the pitch at 22 yards.

The ancient American Indian game of lacrosse involved teams of up to 1,000 players.

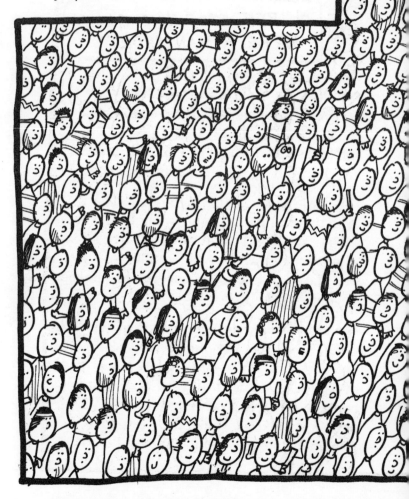

Dr James Naismith invented basketball (or 'indoor rugby', as it was originally called) in 1891 as something to occupy students between the football and baseball seasons. It was one of the game's early players who started calling it basketball because of the peach baskets that acted as the original goals.

In the 13th century the Dutch used to play a game known as *spel metten colve* ('Game played with a club'). This became just *colve*, then *colf* and, eventually, golf.

But that's not the only game for which the Dutch *might* be responsible. Some historians say the Dutch invented baseball. Paintings from the 1600s shows children playing something very similar to the modern game. So it's possible that Dutch settlers may have brought baseball to North America.

Baseball can certainly be traced back to the 18th century. The game was described in a 1744 British book, *A Little Pretty Pocket Book*. There's also a reference to baseball in Jane Austen's 1799 novel *Northanger Abbey*. In the first chapter the young English heroine, Catherine Morland, is described as preferring

'cricket, baseball, riding on horseback and running about the country to books'.

In 1818 Baron Karl von Drais de Sauerbrun (a made-up name if ever I heard one) patented the 'Draisine', the forerunner of the bicycle. The first practical bicycle was the velocipede (built in 1861).

Table tennis was originally played with balls made from champagne corks and paddles made from cigar-box lids. It was created in the 1880s by James Gibb, a British engineer who wanted a game he could play indoors when it was raining. Named 'gossima', the game was first marketed with celluloid balls, which replaced the champagne corks. It became a big seller after the equipment manufacturer renamed the game 'ping-pong' in 1901.

William Webb Ellis is usually credited with the invention of rugby at Rugby School in 1823, when he allegedly caught the ball while playing football and ran towards the opposition goal. It's a good story but not good, correct history. Still, it *is* true to say that Rugby schoolboys helped to develop the

rules for the game.

The first international rugby game was played in 1871 between England and Scotland. It took place at Raeburn Place, Stockbridge, Edinburgh, and Scotland won.

Ten-pin bowling used to be played with nine pins. Then, in colonial Connecticut, a law was passed making 'bowling at nine pins' illegal. So keen bowlers added another pin to make it 'bowling at ten pins' – which was, of course, legal!

Snooker was started by Colonel Sir Neville Chamberlain (no, not the 20th-century Prime Minister) in India in 1875 as a hybrid of pyramids, black pool and billiards. The game was brought over to England some 10 years later.

The name 'snooker' came from the nickname given to cadets at the Royal Military Academy in Woolwich.

Unusual sports

Stoolball is a sport that dates back to the 15th century – or even earlier. It is a cross between cricket, baseball and rounders, and it originated in the southern English county of Sussex, where it's still played (though I confess – to my shame – that as a resident of that county I have never attended a game). It derives its name from the fact that the milkmaids who once played the game used their milking stools as wickets.

Drag racing usually involves two vehicles competing to be the first to cross a finish line, usually from a standing start, and in a straight line. Most drag races take place over an incredibly short distance – perhaps no more than 400 metres – and so are a contest of speed rather than endurance. This means that races last just a few seconds because all the emphasis is on achieving an immense burst of speed – often exceeding 300 mph. In fact, some of the cars are so fast that they actually require a parachute to slow them down! Drag racing started in the US in the 1940s, but as it's grown in popularity, it has spread right across the world.

Sky surfing is a type of skydiving in which contestants wear boards attached to their feet and perform surfing-style aerobatics while they're on the way down. The boards themselves are a cross between snowboards and skateboards. At last, a sport for people for whom parachuting just isn't exciting enough!

Underwater hockey – also called *octopush* (a much more satisfactory name) – is a sport in which players push a puck across the bottom

of a swimming pool into goals. It started in South Africa in the 1960s. In a game requiring agility, stamina and concentration in equal measure, the two teams of six members each have to score goals underwater. This is a lot harder than it might initially sound! Although the players wear flippers (for speed), and also use masks and snorkels for air, they're not wearing diving equipment. This means that they constantly have to rise to just below the surface to breathe before diving down again to gain control of the puck. So not only do you have to be a good hockey player, you also have to be completely at home in the water. I'd love to try it!

You've heard of kitesurfing, where people use kites to propel them forward on water? Well, snowkiting is an outdoor winter sport where people use kite power to glide on snow or ice.

As the name suggests, footvolley is a combination of beach volleyball and football. Basically, it's volleyball, but players must use their feet, heads and chests instead of their hands. I've seen it played, and it's an incredible sport that requires huge stamina, first-rate hand–eye coordination and a lot of core strength. It's very similar to foot tennis (popular in South-East Asia), except that that is a cross between football and tennis (where the ball goes back and forth across a net) rather than football and volleyball (where the ball is also passed between team-mates). Consider also jorkyball, which is a kind of mixture of football and squash.

Korfball – which originated in the Netherlands, where it's still very popular – is a cross between netball and basketball. So far, so unremarkable. What makes it more interesting is the fact that it is played by men and women in the same teams. In fact, each

team of eight must contain four men and four women.

The Iditarod dog-sled race – from Anchorage to Nome, Alaska – commemorates an emergency operation in 1925 to get medical supplies to Nome during a deadly diphtheria epidemic.

Snow Snake is a Native American sport in which two teams throw a polished wooden rod (called a snake because its front end is shaped like a snake's head) as far as possible. Each team gets four chances to throw the snake which, pleasingly, slides at speeds of up to 100 mph down a long curved trail in the snow.

Broomball – which originated in Canada – is a lot like ice hockey but is played with brooms instead of hockey sticks. These brooms aren't the same as you'd find in a garden shed (or in a witch's lair) but have a wooden or aluminium shaft and a rubber-moulded triangular head. Interestingly, players wear special rubber-soled shoes instead of skates, and the ice is prepared in such a way that it is smooth and dry.

Those who consider jogging boring might consider the relatively new sport of joggling. This is running while juggling. Your upper body gets exercised as well as your lower body.

Elephant polo – as played in Nepal, Sri Lanka, India and Thailand – is a variation of polo with elephants instead of horses. Slower, you'd have thought, but perhaps more practical than other variations like rabbit polo, crocodile polo and hedgehog polo.

Parkour is an extraordinary activity that is best described as 'the physical discipline of training to overcome any obstacle within one's path by adapting one's movements to the environment'. Originating in France, parkour requires participants to run along a route, trying to negotiate obstacles as efficiently as possible using skills like jumping and climbing. The object of the exercise is to get from the start to the finish of a route using only your body to overcome obstacles like railings and buildings. Think Spider-Man without the super powers and you've probably got it!

As readers of my recent book *Do Igloos Have Loos?* will know, haggis is a traditional Scottish dish which, typically, consists of a sheep's innards (heart, liver and lungs), minced and mixed with onion, oatmeal, suet, spices and salt and cooked in a sheep's stomach.

As I indicated in the book, this is not a meal that appeals to me, and so I have a lot of time for the sport of haggis hurling which, as the name suggests, involves standing on a whisky barrel and hurling a haggis as far and

as accurately as possible. According to the
rules, the haggis must be edible, which – or
so you would have thought – would render
the whole enterprise impossible as (at least in
my opinion) *no* haggis is edible . . .

Unbelievable (2)

During the 1962 Test match between England and Pakistan at Edgbaston, a mouse stopped play by running around on the pitch.

Michael Jordan, the greatest basketball player of all time, was dropped from his high-school basketball team.

In 1980 the entire Liberian football team was threatened with the firing squad if they lost their match against Gambia. They drew. Works better than a team talk, I'd say!

In the 19th century they kept the grass down at Lord's cricket ground by grazing sheep on it.

Aston Villa played their first ever game in March 1875 against a rugby team called Aston Brook St Mary's. The first half was played under rugby rules, the second under soccer rules. I can find no record of which team won – if indeed either side did!

Table tennis was banned in the Soviet Union from 1930 to 1950 because it was thought to be harmful to the eyes – but nobody ever quite worked out why!

In the Spurs v. Burnley match in 1974, both Mike England and John Pratt scored goals against their team in the first half (i.e. own goals) and goals *for* their team in the second half.

The baseball legend Babe Ruth wore a cabbage leaf under his cap to keep him cool.

In 1991 the Grand National was sponsored by Seagram and, completely coincidentally, the winner was called Seagram. The following year's winner was almost as apt: Party Politics won just five days before the General Election.

In the 1936 Swathling Cup table-tennis match, Alex Ehrlich of Poland and Paneth Farcas of Romania played a two-hour-and-12-minute rally for the first point.

King Carol of Romania selected his country's squad for the 1934 football World Cup.

In 1954 Chelsea were playing Leicester City in

a game they won 3–1. It is their second goal that is of interest to us, for it was an own goal . . . but not just *any* own goal. No, this own goal was officially recorded as a 'shared own goal', as two Leicester City defenders, while trying to clear the ball, both simultaneously kicked it into their own net!

A very fine all-round sportsman named Chris Balderstone once played first-class cricket and professional football on the very same day. On 15 September 1975 he played Championship cricket for Leicestershire against Derbyshire at Chesterfield (11.30 a.m. to 6.30 p.m.), and then soccer for Doncaster Rovers against Brentford at Doncaster (7.30 to 9.10 p.m.).

In 1952 Charlie Tully scored both of Northern Ireland's goals in a 2–2 draw with England, one of them from the corner flag. Tully achieved this feat again the following year for Celtic in a Scottish Cup match against Falkirk. He took a corner and swung the ball directly into the net. The referee, assuming that the ball must have been placed away from the corner spot, ordered Tully to retake it. Tully did so, and once again put the ball in the net directly from the corner.

During a 1993 match played in Paraguay between Sportivo Ameliano and General Caballero, a total of 20 red cards were shown, the most ever!

In a 1997–98 Test match between Pakistan

and South Africa, Mushtaq Ahmed was bowling to Pat Symcox when he knocked back Symcox's middle stump. However, the immense heat had fused the bails together and so they didn't fall. In fact, the middle stump bounced back into place and Symcox continued on his way to his second highest Test score. Sounds hugely unfair to me!

In 2003 Sunderland, at home to Charlton Athletic, scored three own goals in just over half an hour! Stephen Wright put through his own goal after 24 minutes, Mark Proctor did so after 29 minutes and then again in the 31st minute. Statistics showed that Charlton were leading 3–0 without having had a single shot on target.

More athletes than spectators attended the 1900 Paris Olympic Games.

In 1922–23 Southampton finished mid-table in Division Two (what would now be the Championship); their record read: won 14, drawn 14, lost 14, goals for: 40, goals against: 40, 42 points from 42 matches. During the season Southampton were awarded four penalties and conceded four penalties. Now *that's* what you call a truly average season!

In the 1986 football World Cup the Portuguese team went on strike (because of training conditions and the way there were treated by their bosses) during the competition. The players refused to train between their first and second games and were eliminated after losing their final group match.

During a 1936 match between Chesterfield and Burnley, the Chesterfield striker Walter Ponting fired a shot which beat the

opposition goalkeeper, only for the ball to burst and fail to cross the goal-line.

As anyone who's seen the film *Invictus* will know, against all the odds South Africa won the 1995 rugby World Cup versus New Zealand. What the film didn't show was that the All Blacks were suffering from food poisoning during the final. Not unreasonably, they blamed this food poisoning on their South African hosts. Unbelievable or believable? You decide!

In 1973 three Notts County players missed the same penalty in a game against Portsmouth. The original penalty was missed but was ordered to be retaken because the goalkeeper had moved (an offence back then, as goalkeepers were obliged to stand absolutely still). The second attempt, by a different player, was also missed, but the referee ordered it to be retaken because he adjudged that a Portsmouth player had encroached into the penalty area. The third attempt, by a third Notts County player, was placed wide of the goal.

During the ancient Olympic Games, all wars between the Greek city states were put on hold until they were finished.

Jim Thorpe, a part-Native American, became a hero when he won gold medals in 1912 for decathlon and pentathlon. However, in 1913 it was revealed that in 1909 and 1910 he had earned $25 a week playing minor league baseball. This infringed his amateur status and he was stripped of his medals by the Amateur Athletic Union. In 1951 Thorpe was portrayed by Burt Lancaster in the film *Jim Thorpe – All-American*. In 1982 the IOC lifted the ban on Thorpe, and the following year, 30 years after his death, his gold medals were given to his children.

The Italian Abdon Pamich won gold for the 50km walk in the 1964 Games, but only after stopping at 38km to throw up.

Melvin Sheppard, the American athlete who won gold in the 800 metres, 1,500 metres and medley relay in the 1908 Olympics, had applied to become a policeman but was rejected – due to a 'weak heart'. He went on to win another three Olympic gold medals. I think we'd all like a heart as weak as that!

In the final of the 3,000m steeplechase at the 1932 Olympics, Volmari Iso-Hollo of

Finland crossed the finishing line with a 40-metre lead. But because the lap checker had forgotten to change the lap counter after the first lap, there was no tape on the line and the lap counter read '1'. So Iso-Hollo set off on another lap and duly won the race by 75 metres in a race which was, by default, extended to 3,400 metres!

Four Boeing 747 jumbo jets could have fitted side by side in the Olympic Stadium in Sydney, Australia.

Cricketing dismissals and ducks

There are 10 ways in which a batsman can get out in cricket: caught, bowled, leg before wicket (LBW), run out, stumped, handling the ball, obstructing the field, hit the ball twice, hit wicket, and timed out. He can also retire. The first five are by far the most common. In Test cricket, for example, only seven batsmen have ever been out for handling the ball, and only one (Sir Len Hutton) for obstruction of the field. No Test batsman has ever been dismissed for hitting the ball twice or been timed out. By the way, a batsman is allowed to hit the ball a second time if it's threatening to hit his stumps, but not for any other reason.

It's bad enough to be out first ball, but it's even worse if that first ball also happens to be the very first ball of a Test match. This happens very rarely: in fact just 28 times in Test history. At the time of writing, the most recent batsman to be out on the very first ball of a Test match was England's Andrew Strauss against South Africa in 2010.

You probably know that a batsman who is dismissed without scoring (i.e. for no runs) is said to have scored a 'duck'. This is supposedly because a duck's egg looks like a zero. There are a few variations on this theme:

A golden duck is when a player is dismissed on the very first ball he faces.

If he doesn't even face a ball – probably because he was run out coming from the non-striker's end – it's called a diamond duck.

If a player is out on the very first ball of the season, it's called a platinum duck!

If a player is dismissed for nought in both innings of the same two-innings match, it's called a 'pair'.

If a player is dismissed *first ball* in both innings, it's called a 'king pair'.

37 batsmen have been dismissed for a pair on their debuts in Test cricket – including England's Graham Gooch, who went on to have a very distinguished career as a batsman.

Only 11 players in the history of Test cricket have been out for king pairs (i.e. first ball in both innings), including Australia's great batsman (and wicketkeeper) Adam Gilchrist.

The New Zealand bowler Chris Martin has six

Test pairs to his name, having been dismissed without scoring in both innings in six Test matches, two more than any other player.

With a Test batting average of 2.28 (at the time of writing), Chris Martin might be called the ultimate 'rabbit' (as poor batsmen – i.e. people who are in the side purely for their bowling – are known).

If we were being very cruel – perish the thought! – we might even describe him as a 'ferret'. Why? Because the ferret goes in after the rabbits (think about it!).

Perhaps we ought to settle for the the expression 'walking wicket'.

Shirt dedications

Some football clubs dedicate a (shirt) number to their fans, and therefore don't give that shirt number to any of their players. The most common choice as the fans' number is 12. This is because fans are often collectively described as 'the twelfth man'. Clubs and teams reserving the number 12 for their supporters include: Aberdeen, Bristol City, Bristol Rovers, Oxford United, Plymouth Argyle, Portsmouth, Scunthorpe United and Stockport County.

Reading and Norwich City reserve the number 13 for their supporters. AFC Bournemouth use the number 32 for theirs, while Oldham Athletic use the number 40 for theirs.

It's a nice gesture, but my own feeling is that fans would rather be given something to cheer about on the pitch . . .

None of a kind

Anyone who's ever done PE will know all about gyms (or gymnasiums, to give them their full name). The first gyms were in ancient Greece, and what clothing did they wear? None at all – which must have made rope-climbing especially hazardous . . .

No high jumper has ever been able to stay off the ground for longer than a second.

No women competed at the first modern Olympic Games because the Games' founder, Baron Pierre de Coubertin, felt that their inclusion would be 'impractical, uninteresting, unaesthetic and incorrect'! How wrong could a man be!

When it comes to the rugby World Cup, no Australian or South African side has ever lost in the final. No French side, on the other hand, has ever won in the final – despite making two appearances.

The first game in each of the football World Cups of 1966, 1970, 1974 and 1978 finished in a goalless draw. In other words, there were no goals scored in 360 minutes of football. As in most World Cups, the 2010 World Cup also started with a draw, but at least it was a 1–1 draw!

In 1913 the rugby union player W. J. A. Davies began his 22-cap England career. In all that time, he never finished on the losing side.

None of the following sports were included in the first modern Olympics (in 1896): rowing, hockey, equestrianism, soccer, yachting, boxing, archery, basketball or modern pentathlon.

Esha Ness won the Grand National that never was. It was in 1993, when the race was declared void after many of the riders didn't hear the starter's recall. The first horse past the post was Esha Ness, ridden by John White, but the victory didn't count.

Tour de France jerseys

The Tour de France is an annual 2,200-mile cycle race that is widely acknowledged as the toughest sporting contest in the world. It's also called the Greatest Free Show on Earth!

You might know that the leading rider (overall) wears the yellow jersey. But there are also other jerseys. The green jersey is awarded for sprint points – at the end of each stage, points are earned by the riders who finish first, second, etc.

The polka-dot jersey is awarded to the rider who earns the most points at each summit of a hill or pass. The winner is known as the King of the Mountains.

The white jersey is given to the leading young rider (overall) – i.e. a competitor aged less than 26 years as of 1 January of that year.

Records

Every sport has lots of records. Obviously I can't list them all here or this book would run to several thousand pages. So here's a selection of some of the more interesting ones.

The heaviest sumo wrestler, Konishiki – known as the Dump Truck – weighed 630 pounds (286kg). He was once said to have drunk more than 100 beers and eaten 70 pieces of sushi in a single meal.

Grimsby Town hold the dubious record of having been relegated more times than any other English club.

The world's longest competitive tennis match took place at Wimbledon in 2010, when the American player John Isner beat the Frenchman Nicolas Mahut after playing for 11 hours and five minutes over three days. The reason it went on so long is because in the final set, a player must win by two clear games (there is no tie break, as there are in previous sets). The score in their final set was

70–68 – that's 138 games played over eight hours 11 minutes – making it the longest set in history in both time and games. What an extraordinary match – and what a shame that both players couldn't have gone through to the next round!

At the age of 101, Larry Lewis ran the 100 yards in 17.8 seconds – setting a new world record for runners of 100 or older.

The record for the most Olympic medals ever won is held by the Soviet gymnast Larissa Latynina. Competing in three Olympics between 1956 and 1964, she won 18 medals – including nine golds.

The American swimmer Michael Phelps holds the record for the most Olympic *gold* medals: 14, with the possibility of more to come in 2012. He also holds the record for the most gold medals won in a single Olympics: his eight at the 2008 Beijing Games eclipsed his fellow-American swimmer Mark Spitz's seven golds at the 1972 Munich Games.

At the time of writing, Phelps has won 16 Olympic medals: six gold and two bronze at Athens in 2004, and eight golds at Beijing in 2008. In doing so he has twice equalled the record eight medals (of any type) at a single Olympics achieved by the Russian gymnast Alexander Dityatin in 1980.

Norway has won more medals at the Winter Olympic Games than any other nation. The

Norwegians have won 303 (107 of which were gold); their nearest rivals, the US, have won 253 (87 of which were gold).

However, with 2,296 medals (929 gold), the US easily holds the record for the most medals in the Summer Olympics, with more than double the medals of their nearest competitor (the old Soviet Union, with 1,010). Great Britain comes a very respectable third with 715.

The longest tandem – i.e. extended bicycle – was designed for 35 riders. It was 20 metres long and weighed as much as a small car.

The smallest bicycle that an adult could ride had wheels made from silver dollars.

The quickest booking in a Football League/ Premiership match was after just *five* seconds. The culprit? Vinnie Jones, playing for Sheffield United against Manchester City. He was booked again later in the match and was therefore sent off.

The world record for balancing people on your head is 92 in an hour (though why anyone should want to achieve such a record is another matter).

Arsenal have been in the top flight of football (the Premier League/old Division One) without a break since 1919. That's longer than any other club.

In 1920 the French tennis player Suzanne Lenglen won all three Wimbledon titles (the singles, the doubles and the mixed doubles) without dropping a single set.

Table tennis is the world's biggest participation sport.

Geoff Allott of New Zealand batted for 101 minutes before being dismissed for a duck against South Africa at Auckland in 1999. It's a record, but I very much doubt that many

cricketers will seek to beat it!

In 1996 a group of golfers achieved the fastest round by a team when they completed all 18 holes at the Tatnuck Country Club in just nine minutes and 28 seconds.

Female tennis players are notorious for grunting when they hit the ball. Maria Sharapova's shriek was measured at 101 decibels, which is as loud as a police car siren.

In motor racing, the hat trick of gaining pole position, winning the race and achieving the fastest lap is known as 'the perfect race'. At the time of writing, the German driver Michael Schumacher has had 22 such perfect races – precisely twice the number of his nearest competitor, Britain's Jim Clark.

The Australian racing driver Mark Webber holds the unenviable record of the most races before achieving his first Grand Prix win. When he won the 2009 German Grand Prix, it was his 130th race (seven races more than it took Rubens Barrichello to win his first). Mind you, Britain's Jenson Button wasn't too quick off the mark: he had to wait until his 113th race (the 2006 Hungarian Grand Prix) before he could take the chequered flag.

But if Mark Webber's record is unenviable, what does that make Andrea de Cesaris's? The Italian driver holds the record for the most races without a win: 214. Poor fellow – the other drivers should have let him win one . . .

Sport around the world

A game popular with young people in Afghanistan is 'kite fighting'. The kite strings are covered with a mixture of flour and powdered glass, and participants try to cut through the strings of their opponents' kites.

Wrestling is also popular in Afghanistan. The object of the game is to pin your opponent to the ground without touching his legs.

Before we leave Afghanistan, let me draw your attention to a game called *gursai* that is played in the countryside: players have to hold their left foot in their right hand and hop around trying to knock each other over.

The Bangkok Golf Club is floodlit so it is possible to play 24 hours a day.

There's an official snowball-throwing contest in Sweden.

Dutch farmers learned a kind of pole-vaulting so they could cross drainage ditches and get from field to field. This became a sport called *polsstokspringen*.

Yukigassen (a Japanese word which when translated means 'snow battle') is a sport that started in Japan but is also popular in Finland, Norway and Australia. Two teams with seven players each chuck snow at each other on a court with specific measurements. Sounds fun!

In Albania, a traditional sport for women is competitive mountain climbing against the clock.

Brazil has more professional soccer teams than any other country in the world.

Chess is so popular in Armenia it is practically the national sport!

One sport played at festivals in the desert regions of Algeria requires riders on horses travelling at a full gallop to shoot at a target, before bringing their mounts to a complete stop. Another tradition during festivals is camel dancing, in which riders direct their camels to move to the beat of traditional music.

Canada's official national sports are ice hockey (in the winter) and lacrosse (in the summer).

Every August, an unusual race is held in the Australian Outback near Alice Springs. It's called the Henley-on-Todd boat race, but it's a boat race with a difference. Because water is rarely found in the Todd River, competitors must carry their boats along the dry river bed.

Burmese boxing is a violent sport in which the victor is the one who draws first blood.

Cycling is the number one sport in Belgium, which has hundreds of miles of cycle paths.

The only European countries where football isn't the most popular spectator sport are Ireland (Gaelic football is the top sport), Finland (ice hockey), and Latvia and Estonia (both basketball).

Buzkashi, which literally means 'goat-grabbing', is a popular sport in Central Asian countries. It dates as far back as the 13th century. Here's how it works: the players are all on horseback and they have to ride around a pit that contains a dead calf. They're all trying to pick it up, and once one of them has done so, he has to drop it into the 'Circle of Justice'- the goal. The other riders have to try and stop him. Anyone can be the winner. The only loser is the calf . . .

Finland is home to a sport named *pesäpallo*. It's a summer sport played in rural areas and small towns and it's very similar to baseball.

The Paraguayan football team speaks the

indigenous language of Guarani on the pitch so that the opposing team can't work out what they're saying.

Kabaddi is the national sport of Bangladesh, but it's also popular throughout South-East Asia. In *kabaddi*, two teams occupy opposite halves of a field and take turns sending a 'raider' into the other half to win points by tagging or wrestling members of the opposing team. The raider then tries to return to his own half, holding his breath during the whole raid. Each team consists of 12 players (seven on the field with five in reserve). It's an exhausting game so there are just two 20-minute halves. The British Army now plays the game as part of its training.

In 1969 there was a week-long war between El Salvador and Honduras. It was called the Soccer War because it started at a football match. Of course, the football riot was just the trigger for tension that had built up between the two countries for a couple of years, but a lot of people thought that the war was just over a football match. Incidentally, it was a World Cup qualifying match, which El Salvador won. It wasn't worth a war, though, because they both ended up getting knocked out in the first round of the 1970 World Cup.

A hole in one

In golf, a hole in one (also known as an ace) is when a player hits the ball directly from the tee into the hole with just one shot.

Holes-in-one are rare, but when they do occur, they almost always happen on shorter, par three, holes rather than on longer, par four or par five, holes. Though, having said that, my friend Joel hit a hole in one on a par four, which meant that not only had he recorded an ace but also a much rarer *albatross* (three under par on a hole).

Although professional and top amateur golfers are more likely to achieve holes-in-one, they are often a matter of luck (with the ball hitting a tree or an obstruction before making its way into the hole) and so even total beginners can get one.

Be careful what you wish for, though! It is the custom at almost all golf clubs for the lucky golfer to celebrate his or her achievement by buying drinks for all the other members (or at least for all the other players in the club bar).

In Japan, they prize holes-in-one so highly that when they get them, they send presents to all their friends. It is for this reason that many Japanese golfers carry hole in one insurance – no, honestly! – because the cost of celebrating what they (slightly confusingly)

call an 'albatross' can often cost thousands of pounds.

The longest hole in one was hit by Robert Mitera in 1965 at the Miracle Hills Golf Club in Omaha, Nebraska. Although unable to see the flag from the tee, Mitera drove the ball 444 yards straight into the hole. In fact, Mitera only realized he'd aced the hole when he arrived at the green and another golfer told him that his ball had dropped in.

The youngest boy to hit a hole in one was three-year-old Jake Paine in 2001 in California (by contrast, Tiger Woods was six when he hit his first ace).

The youngest girl to hit a hole in one was five-year-old Eleanor Gamble in 2010 in Cambridge.

The oldest player to hit a hole in one was Harold Stilson, aged 101, in 2001. In the 1973 (British) Open, the great Gene Sarazen made a hole in one at the age of 71.

The chances of one person making two holes-in-one in a round of golf are about 1 in 67 million. Yet in 2010 75-year-old Peter

Wafford did just that – making him the only person ever to achieve such a feat.

That's interesting (4)

The Danish football star Michael Laudrup was part of the great 1990s Barcelona team that beat Real Madrid 5–0. He transferred to Real, and was then a member of the Real Madrid team that beat Barcelona 5–0.

In ancient Greece, a boxing match began with two boxers standing face to face, their noses touching.

Twickenham is where the England rugby union team play all their home games. During the First World War, horses, cows and sheep grazed on the pitch. During the Second World War, one car park was dug up for allotments to grow vegetables and the other was used as a coal dump.

The most isolated ground in the Football/ Premier Leagues belongs to Carlisle United, who are 58 miles from their nearest neighbour, Newcastle United. At the opposite end of the scale, up in Scotland, Dundee and Dundee United are only some 200 metres apart.

In horse races, the favourite wins just under 30 per cent of the time.

The 1982 football World Cup threw up some very strange statistics. England were eliminated without being defeated (in play) during their five games. Italy advanced from the first group stage with three draws in three games – precisely the same record as Cameroon, who were eliminated on the basis of having scored fewer goals than Italy. However, in their game against Peru,

the Cameroonian striker Roger Milla had a
goal disallowed for offside when TV replays
showed that he was clearly *onside*. If the
goal had been given, Cameroon would have
progressed at the expense of Italy who, in
fact, went on to win the whole tournament.

In 1946 the French tennis player Yvon Petra
was extremely fortunate to find himself
playing at Wimbledon – or, indeed, anywhere.
He had been seriously wounded during the
war and seemed likely to lose his leg but for
the skill of a German surgeon (he had been
captured), who saved the limb. Incredibly,
Petra recovered from that injury and not only
competed at Wimbledon in 1946 but actually
won that year's men's singles!

Gymnasts sometimes use golden syrup
instead of talcum powder for a better grip on
the parallel bars.

Many cricket fans know that in 1926 the
Australian state team Victoria scored a record
total of 1,107 runs in a home game against
New South Wales in Melbourne. What most
people *don't* know is that in the return match
(at NSW's home ground in Sydney), Victoria

were bowled out for just 35 runs.

Eddie Arcaro, one of the greatest jockeys in the history of American horse racing, rode 250 losers before winning his first race.

In the early 1980s Southampton's line-up contained six past, present or future England captains: Alan Ball, Mick Channon, Kevin Keegan, Mick Mills, Peter Shilton and Dave Watson.

AC Milan was founded in 1899 by a British man named Alfred Edwards – and that's why they call themselves Milan (the English version of the city's name) rather than the Italian 'Milano'.

Arsenal won the Championship in 1937–38 with 52 points – just 16 more than the club that finished bottom.

When a baseball is hit really hard, it momentarily changes shape by as much as 25 per cent.

Americans spend more than $630 million a year on golf balls.

Bobby Moore was England's captain when

they won the 1966 football World Cup. He played for West Ham United but his middle name was Chelsea.

Sporting superstitions

Sportsmen and -women train so hard and prepare so well for their sports that it's little surprise that many are also highly superstitious. If you've done all that you can possibly do before a big game or event (i.e. all the 'proper' preparation) and you're still not convinced that you're going to win, then you'll probably be tempted to turn to less rational things like luck and superstition.

Sports psychologists reckon that successful sportsmen and -women tend, by nature, to be at least slightly obsessive. The same compulsive nature that gives them the drive to keep on practising to the very utmost of their ability can also lead them to adopt rituals that often seem rather strange to observers.

SPORTING PERSONALITIES AND THEIR SUPERSTITIONS

Footballer Kolo Toure has a (quite common) superstition about always being the last player out of the dressing room. In 2009, however, it got him into trouble. Playing for

Arsenal, he found himself waiting for team-mate William Gallas to receive treatment during the interval so that he could leave the dressing room last. Alas for Toure, Gallas took longer than expected, and when they both missed the start of the second half, Toure was given a yellow card.

The former England footballer Paul Ince was another player who insisted on being the last to leave the dressing room. This was fine until he found himself playing alongside someone with the same superstition . . . chaos ensued.

Tiger Woods always wears a red T-shirt on the last day of a golfing tournament. He does this because his mother told him that red represents power. All the tournaments that Woods has won while wearing red on the final day have only served to reinforce this superstition.

The British diver Tom Daley, who became Britain's second youngest Olympian when he competed in the 2008 Beijing Olympics, takes his beloved toy monkey with him to all his competitions – placing him in sight of the diving board.

The now retired Croatian tennis player Goran Ivanišević was incredibly superstitious. During a match he would avoid stepping on the court lines and always tried to be the second player up from his seat following a break. Away from the court, he was even more superstitious.

When he won a match, he would repeat everything he did the previous day, such as eating the same food at the same restaurant, talking to the same people and watching the same TV programmes. The year he won Wimbledon 2001, this meant he found himself watching *Teletubbies* every morning. 'Sometimes it got very boring,' he confessed.

The Australian racing driver Alexander Wurz had a strange superstition: whenever he raced, he always wore one red and one blue shoe.

The former England Test wicketkeeper Jack Russell refused to change his hat or wicketkeeping pads throughout his career, so by the time he retired they were falling apart and very, *very* smelly. He'd also use just a single tea bag for a whole five-day Test

– hanging the tea bag out to dry between cuppas. He also ate two Weetabix for lunch every day, which might sound fair enough – except he insisted that the cereal was soaked in milk for precisely eight minutes.

The England footballer John Terry has admitted to having 'about 50' pre-match superstitions – including sitting in the same seat on the team bus, listening to the same CD and parking in the same spot in the car park. He also wore the same 'lucky' shin guards for more than a decade. However, before a 2004 Champions League tie in Barcelona, he lost them. Terry and Chelsea went on to lose the match. Later he said, 'Those shin-pads had got me to where I was in the game . . . I've had those shin-pads for so long and now this is it, all over.'

The South African opening batsman Neil McKenzie used to have many rituals – including taping his bat to the ceiling before each innings and insisting that every toilet seat in the dressing room was down when he went out to bat. He himself has said of his actions, 'I think it was obsessive compulsive disorder. It was a disease. It was not just cricket, it was life in general. You've got numbers that you like, things that you like . . . it's a ritual, trying to control what you can't control. I've never had superstitions about ladders or black cats. It was OCD. I've cut it out now. I've got a wife and child now and don't have much time to worry about toilet seats and taping bats to the ceiling.'

The French footballer Laurent Blanc always kissed the top of a bald man's head before every game.

Tennis star Serena Williams revealed her superstitions after failing to win a tournament. 'I didn't tie my laces right and I didn't bounce the ball five times and I didn't bring my shower sandals to the court with me. I didn't have my extra dress. I just knew fate, it wasn't going to happen.'

Onlys (2)

Robert Prosineki is the only player to have scored for two different countries at the football World Cup finals. He scored for Yugoslavia in 1990 before changing to become a Croatian national and scoring for them in 1998.

The Open Championship is one of the four major golf championships and is held annually in the UK. As the world's oldest golf championship, it's only one that doesn't have to put its nationality or venue in the title.

Only two Test matches have ever been tied – the first between West Indies and Australia in Brisbane in 1960–61 and the second between Australia and India in Madras in 1986–87.

In the history of professional boxing, only four men have been knocked out in the first 11 seconds of the first round.

Swansea City are the only League club to have had four pairs of brothers on their playing staff at the same time.

Only two members of FIFA – France and Belgium – actually participated in the first football World Cup; while only four countries participated in all of the first three World Cups: Romania, Brazil, France and Belgium. Only eight different countries have won the World Cup: Argentina, Brazil, England, France, Germany, Italy, Spain and Uruguay.

In 1982 Duleep Mendis of Sri Lanka scored 105 in both innings of a Test match against India – making him the only batsman to hit identical hundreds in both innings of a Test.

There are only two sports in which teams have to move backwards to win: tug-of-war and rowing. You can make that three if you include a backstroke relay race.

Sam Wynne is the only footballer to have scored two goals for *each* side in a single first-class game. It happened in a match between his team, Oldham Athletic, and Manchester United in the 1923–24 season. He scored two goals for Oldham and two own goals. It didn't matter as his team ended up winning 5–2.

In 1983 the British racing driver John Watson became the only driver to win a Formula One Grand Prix from as far back as 22nd on the grid.

Plenty of men have played Test cricket for two countries, but John Traicos is the only man to be born in one country and then play Test cricket for two other countries. He was born in Egypt, played Test cricket for South Africa in 1970 and then for Zimbabwe more than 22 years later, when they were awarded Test status in 1992.

Maurice Turnbull was the only man to play cricket for England and hockey and rugby for Wales. He also won the South Wales Squash Championship. Tragically, he was killed in the Second World War.

The only person to have played both World Cup football and World Cup cricket is Viv Richards – for Antigua at football and for the West Indies at cricket.

Lala Amarnath and Surinder Amarnath are the only father and son to both score Test centuries on debut. Incredibly, neither scored another Test century.

In 1971 golf became the only sport to have
been played on the moon when astronaut
Alan Shepard hit a golf ball. Despite wearing
thick gloves and a spacesuit that forced him
to swing the club with just one hand, Shepard
struck two golf balls, driving the second
'miles and miles and miles'.

There have only been two drawn matches in the history of the rugby World Cup, one involving France and Scotland in 1987 and another between Canada and Japan in 2007.

Jonny Wilkinson is the only player in the history of the rugby World Cup to have scored points in two World Cup finals.

The discus is the only track-and-field event in which a men's world record has never been set during the Olympic Games.

The Ashes

When England plays Australia in Test cricket, they're said to be playing for 'the Ashes'. You might be surprised to know that they really *are* playing for ashes!

It all started in 1882, when Australia beat England on an English ground for the first time. A notice appeared in the *Sporting Times* which read: *In Affectionate Remembrance of English Cricket, which died at The Oval on 29th August, 1882. Deeply lamented by a large circle of sorrowing friends and acquaintances. RIP. NB – The body will be cremated and the ashes taken to Australia.*

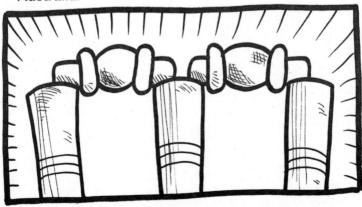

This was obviously meant as a joke, but when England went to tour Australia the next year, the newspapers wrote about 'the quest to regain the Ashes'. And while the England team were in Melbourne, the captain was presented with a small terracotta urn containing some ashes. What those ashes were made of isn't actually known – a bail? A stump? Even a lady's veil? – but there *are* ashes, and the little urn that contains them is contested in Test series between the two nations.

The Ashes, which are kept on permanent display at Lord's cricket ground, are currently held by England.

Giant-killing feats in football

South Africa 2, France 1 (2010)
Egypt 1, Italy 0 (2009)
Senegal 1, France 0 (2002)
Wrexham 2, Arsenal 1 (1992)
West Bromwich Albion 2, Woking 4 (1991)
Cameroon 1, Argentina 0 (1990)
Sutton 2, Coventry City 1 (1989)
Wimbledon 1, Liverpool 0
(1988 – FA Cup final)
Birmingham City 1, Altrincham 2 (1986)
AFC Bournemouth 2, Manchester United 0
(1984)
Algeria 2, West Germany 1 (1982)
Exeter City 4, Newcastle United 0 (1981)
Harlow 1, Leicester City 0 (1980)
Colchester United 3, Leeds United 2 (1971)
North Korea 1, Italy 0 (1966)
Everton 1, Leyton Orient 3 (1952)
USA 1, England 0 (1950)
Yeovil Town 2, Sunderland 1 (1949)

Keepie uppie

Keepie uppie is the art of juggling a football using your feet, knees, legs, chest and head without allowing the ball to hit the ground.

The men's record for the longest keepie uppie was set by Briton Dan Magness, who kept a football off the ground for 24 hours at London's Covent Garden in May 2009. No one was counting, but it was estimated that he hit the ball 250,000 times. The record he broke had been set in August 2003 by Brazilian Martinho Eduardo Orige, who kept a football in the air for 19 hours and 30 minutes.

The women's record was set in July 1996 by Brazilian Cláudia Martin, who managed seven hours and five minutes.

Dan Magness set another keepie-uppie record in January 2010 when he walked 30 miles doing keepie uppie without letting the ball touch the ground. On his journey, he visited all the Premier League stadiums in London, starting his journey at Fulham's

Craven Cottage and ending it at Tottenham
Hotspur's White Hart Lane.

Jan Skorkovsky ran the 1990 Prague Marathon in seven hours 18 minutes 55 seconds while doing keepie uppie – again without the ball ever touching the ground.

However, the most famous display of keepie uppie was probably in the 1967 England v. Scotland international. Scotland were leading 3–2 against the World Cup holders, and the Scottish midfielder 'Slim' Jim Baxter tauntingly played keepie uppie in front of the English defence in order to waste time and, yes, to show off his incredible skills. It is many Scottish football fans' favourite sporting moment! This Englishman enjoyed it too!

Football substitutes

Substitutions were first allowed in English League matches in the 1965–66 season, with Keith Peacock the first substitute to be used when he came on for Charlton Athletic against Bolton on 21 August 1965.

In the same month, Bob Knox became the first substitute to score a League goal when he came on for Barrow against Wrexham. Coincidentally, later that season Knox replaced an injured goalkeeper and became the first substitute to save a penalty.

In that first season, a player could only be substituted if he'd been injured. However, at the end of the season the League decided that it was impossible for the referee to decide when a player was genuinely injured and so substitutions were soon allowed for tactical reasons.

Substitutes were allowed in the World Cup finals for the first time in 1970.

In 1982 László Kiss of Hungary became the

first substitute ever to score a hat trick in a
World Cup match.

The quickest substitution in a League match
was in a 1983 tie between Chester and
Darlington. Colin Ross injured his knee at
the kick-off and Darlington were obliged
to substitute him after just *five* seconds. In
1973 Brian Hornsby of Arsenal came on as a
substitute for the last *three* seconds of the
game against Manchester United.

The most pointless substitution of all time?
It has to be Emile Heskey (a fine player but
not a great goalscorer) for Jermain Defoe (a
proven goalscorer) when England were 4–1
down against Germany in the World Cup
2010. I know, I know, I really must get over
it . . .

Just for fun

SOME WAYS IN WHICH WE BRITS WILL ALWAYS TRIUMPH AT WIMBLEDON

Receiving the most wild card entries

Cheering giant TV screens

Quaffing champagne in hospitality tents

Queueing

Charging over the odds for strawberries

Rain commentaries

Accepting dodgy line calls

Losing gracefully

WONDERFULLY PUNNY SPORTS STARS' AUTOBIOGRAPHIES

By George (boxer George Foreman)

Life Swings (golfer Nick Faldo – a golfer swings)

Gray Matters (footballer Andy Gray – a pun on 'grey matter', as brains are also known)

Big Fry (football manager Barry Fry)

Watt's My Name (boxer Jim Watt)

Managing My Life (football manager Alex Ferguson)

No Holding Back (cricketer Michael Holding)

Heading for Victory (footballer Steve Bruce)

Nine Lives (rugby union player Matt Dawson – an ex-scrum half who wore the number nine shirt)

It's All About a Ball (footballer Alan Ball)

Right Back to the Beginning (footballer Jimmy Armfield – who played right-back)

Hell Razor (footballer Neil Ruddock – who had the nickname Razor)

Maine Man (footballer Tony Book – an ex-player with Manchester City, who play their home games at Maine Road)

Banks of England (footballer Gordon Banks)

Playing for Keeps (cricketer Alec Stewart – a wicketkeeper)

The Real Mackay (footballer Dave Mackay – a pun on the expression 'the Real McCoy')

A GUIDE TO RUGBY UNION POSITIONS

Stand-off – Someone who is too aloof to join the scrum

Conversion – Recipient of corporate hospitality finds that he actually *enjoys* the game

Scrum – Absolutely *no* chance of getting to the bar at half-time

Ruck – What would be illegal off the field is perfectly legal on it

Kick-off – The attempt to part a player and his head (see also Ruck)

Second Row – . . . and the game's only just started

Overlap – What happens to a forward's belly when he retires from the sport

Big Hit – Former player who finds himself winning a TV celebrity talent contest

Maul – Only for British Lions

No. 8 – We won – who's counting?

Prop – What players do to the bar after the game

Sidestep – What international players must do to avoid fans at the end of a game

THE RULES OF CRICKET

You have two sides, one out in the field and one in.

Each man that's in the side that's in goes out, and when he's out he comes in and the next man goes in until he's out.

ADVANCED
UNIVERSITY
COURSES
° NUCLEAR THERMODYNAMICS
• QUANTUM MECHANICS
• BRAIN SURGERY
• RULES OF CRICKET *
• EXISTENTIALISM
• POST MODERNISM
*DOES NOT COVER THE LBW LAW.

When a man goes out to go in, the men who are out try to get him out, and when he is out he goes in and the next man in goes out and goes in.

When they are all out, the side that's out comes in and the side that's been in goes out and tries to get those coming in, out.

Sometimes there are men still in and not out.

There are two men called umpires who stay out all the time and they decide when the men who are in are out.

When both sides have been in and all the men are out (including those who are not out), then the game is finished.

A hypnotist named Romark used his supposed skills on some of the Southport players during the 1975–76 football season, after the team had lost several games. However, Southport lost their next match 2–1 to Watford . . .

The goalkeeper of Turkish team Orduspor was given a £50 bonus in 1980 after his team lost 4–0. Normally he let in twice as many goals.

Bill Shankly was a great manager of Liverpool. He was so committed to his team that he once said, 'There are only two teams in Liverpool: Liverpool and Liverpool Reserves.' And, no, it didn't go down well with Everton fans! Shanks (as he was known to the world of football) also gave his players a piece of invaluable advice: 'If you're in the penalty area and aren't sure what to do with the ball, just stick it in the net and we'll discuss your options afterwards.' His attitude to the game can be summed up in a single quote: 'Some people think football is a matter of life and death. I don't like that attitude. I can assure them it is much more serious than that.'

In ancient Japan, public contests were held in towns to see who could fart the loudest and longest. Winners were awarded big prizes and received a lot of attention. That's strange: you'd have thought that people would have taken great care to avoid them!

Lewis Carroll invented a strange version of croquet in *Alice in Wonderland*. Players used a flamingo as a mallet, a hedgehog as the ball, and soldiers doubled over to make the hoops!

THINGS THAT HAPPEN EVERY YEAR AT WIMBLEDON

Only one British player makes it through to the second week – unless there's a lot of rain

A lot of rain

The BBC ends its coverage in the middle of the fifth set of an important match

A top tennis player – probably an American – hands his racket over to a ball boy after playing a bad shot

There are daily pictures in the papers of people queueing

There are daily stories in the papers about the scandalous cost of strawberries

There are no upsets in the women's singles

THE WISEST THING EVER SAID ABOUT FOOTBALL

'Football is a game in which a handful of fit men run around for one and a half hours watched by millions of people who could really use the exercise' – Unknown

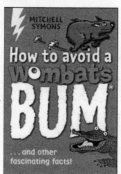

Mitchell Symons
HOW TO AVOID A WOMBAT'S BUM*
And other fascinating facts!

* Don't chase it! Wombats can run up to 25 miles per hour and stop dead in half a stride. They kill their predators this way – the predator runs into the wombat's bum-bone and smashes its face.

Amaze and intrigue your friends and family with more fantastic facts and figures:

- most dinosaurs were no bigger than chickens
- Everton was the first British football club to introduce a stripe down the side of players' shorts
- A snail has about 25,000 teeth
- No piece of paper can be folded in half more than seven times

Just opening this book will have you hooked for hours!

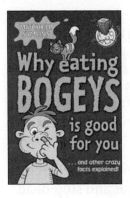

Mitchell Symons
WHY EATING BOGEYS IS GOOD FOR YOU

And other crazy facts explained!

Ever wondered . . .

- Why we have tonsils?
- Is there any cream in cream crackers?
- What's the best way to cure hiccups?
- And if kangaroos keep their babies in their pouches, what happens to all the poo?

Mitchell Symons answers all these wacky questions and plenty more in a wonderfully addictive book that will have you hooked for hours!

(And eating bogeys is good for you . . . but only your own!)

Selected for the Booktrust Booked Up! Initiative in 2008.

Mitchell Symons
HOW MUCH POO
DOES AN
ELEPHANT DO?*

. . . and further fascinating
facts!

* An elephant produces an eye-wateringly
pongy 20 kilograms of dung a day!

Let Mitchell Symons be your guide into the
weird and wonderful world of trivia.

- Camels are born without humps
- Walt Disney, creator of Mickey Mouse, was
  scared of mice
- Only 30% of humans can flare their
  nostrils
- A group of twelve or more cows is called a
  flink

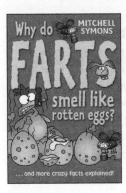

Mitchell Symons
WHY DO FARTS SMELL LIKE ROTTEN EGGS?

. . . and more crazy facts
explained!

Ever wondered . . .

- Why we burp?
- What a wotsit is?
- Whether lemmings really jump off cliffs?
- Why vomit always contains carrots?
- And why *do* farts smell like rotten eggs?

No subject is too strange and no trivia
too tough for Mitchell Symons, who has
the answers to these crazy questions, and
many more.

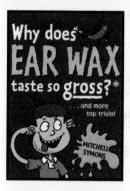

Mitchell Symons

WHY DOES EAR WAX TASTE SO GROSS?*

... and more top trivia!

*stinky ear wax has been hanging around in the ear canal for nearly a month before it is 'pickable'!

Did you know ...

- **Humans share a third of their DNA with lettuce**

- **Cockroaches fart every fifteen minutes**

- **Giraffes never kneel**

- **The average person spends six months of their life on the loo**

Amaze your mates and fascinate your family with this book packed with jaw-dropping, eyebrow-raising facts!

Mitchell Symons

WHY YOU NEED A PASSPORT WHEN YOU'RE GOING TO PUKE*

. . . and more crazy-
but-true facts!

*Puke is the name of a town in Albania.
Would YOU like to holiday there . . . ?

Did you know . . .

- **Square watermelons are sold in Japan**

- **There is a River Piddle in Dorset**

- **American use enough toilet paper
  daily to wrap around the world
  nine times**

Mitchell Symons goes global – join him
on his fun fact-finding world tour!

Q: Who writes the best books on farts, bogeys and other yucky stuff?

A: Mitchell Symons, of course

Q: What's his website called?

A: Grossbooks.co.uk, what else!

On this site you can:
- Win cool stuff in quizzes and competitions
- Add your own fab facts and publish them online
- Be first to find out about Mitchell's new books before they're published

As Mitchell's mum would say:
'Thank goodness it's not *scratch 'n' sniff*...'

See for yourself at **Grossbooks.co.uk**